Travis Agnew has a heart for the Great Comm
reaching non-believers, but also to teaching and
he focuses on helping college students live for C
– the college campus. I encourage college stud
teachings, and strive to be a great witness for Christ!
_____, learn from its

-Chuck Lawless, Dean, Billy Graham School, Vice President for Academic Programming, The Southern Baptist Theological Seminary

I first got to know Travis as a gifted speaker for a Christian youth camp I helped run. I was impressed with his gentle yet direct presentation of the truth of God's Word. I am happy to see that the same voice is heard in the pages of this book. In *Freshman 15*, Travis unapologetically lifts up God's Word as *the* basis for developing a healthy worldview, yet he does so in a way that makes you want to listen. Travis speaks like the campus minister everyone wishes they had – someone who challenges you, who sets a high standard for you, but one whom you always know loves you like crazy. *Freshman 15* will be a great resource for helping college students give priority to all the right things in their college career.

-James Jackson, Editor, Life Truths Sunday School Material for Parents

Freshman 15 is written like the New Testament book of James; it's the truth in blue jeans. It's practical, it's scriptural, and it speaks to the real issues that every college freshman will have to deal with. Easy to understand and hard to ignore - this book is a must read for every Christian college student.

-Jeff Lethco, Senior Pastor, North Side Baptist Church

Freshman 15 is a joy to read. Travis Agnew is one of the finest ministers that I know. Travis has a keen insight into the mind and heart of today's college students. He points students to Jesus with every chapter. The thing that I like is that he takes the time to give college students sound, practical, godly advice. In my opinion, Travis Agnew lives his faith in Jesus Christ and has a genuine desire to help collegians follow the same path of discipleship. I have served on college campuses for nearly thirty years and I have observed no one that has more passion for sharing Jesus with college students than Travis. Make sure that you give this book to college students so that they have the opportunity to grow and follow Jesus.

-Scott M. Smith, Campus Minister, Lander University

Wow! It is so refreshing to read a book that biblically addresses fifteen vital areas with the wisdom of Scriptures. At North Greenville University, we want to be a place where Christ makes the difference and *Freshman 15* does a great job of showing how students can have Jesus Christ make the difference through their lives. It will certainly help our students understand better how to give weight to Jesus and live life at the university the way he intended. I have known Travis Agnew since he arrived at North Greenville University as a student in August 1999. Over the years, I have seen him grow physically, socially, mentally, and especially, spiritually. He indeed did not merely survive the university experience as a Christian, but he thrived through it and established the foundation of a real passion for Jesus Christ. Therefore, he now wants to share it all with others and I for one am so very glad that he has. I believe that you will be as well.

-James B. Epting, President of North Greenville University

May I commend to you *Freshman 15*. This primer for college students' spiritual introduction to college life is a must read for college students who want to be a success in college in the most important of ways. Travis Agnew speaks from experience and a heart of ministry for students, many of whom choose the wrong path during these formative years. As you read this book, you will be confronted by the claims of God for your life and will find ways to experience spiritual victory in the midst of a challenging environment. I commend this book to you without hesitation.

-Dr. Frank S. Page, President, Southern Baptist Convention 2006-2008, Senior Pastor, Taylors First Baptist Church

Your life can become a powerful signatured life-masterpiece of God's design. *Freshman 15* strategically and practically reveals what your focus points should be for this to become a reality during your college years. Every collegian or college-bound student who cares about life-impact and eventual legacy should read this book!

-Dwight Robertson, Speaker, Author, and Founding President/CEO of Kingdom Building Ministries, Denver, CO

Travis Agnew knows how to put on weight where it counts! His ability to communicate and illustrate makes this an enjoyable and profitable read for any Christian student. Travis takes the Gospel and the call of the Christian life seriously. If your looking for something worth talking about with a friend over a cup of coffee as you begin life away from home as a Christian, this book will do nicely.

-Paul G. Patrick, Chaplain and Campus Minister, Erskine College and Theological Seminary

My friend Travis Agnew is one of a kind. He is a rare combination of leadership and humility that make him a unique voice for today's generation. I lived up close and personal with Travis for several years during college. He lived the concepts that he has written about. In fact, I don't know anyone who had a more effective college ministry and walk with God than Travis Agnew. I commend him to you as someone who not only understands but has applied the principles in this book.

-Pastor Steven Furtick, Lead Pastor, Elevation Church

It was my joy to know and work with Travis Agnew during his student days at North Greenville University. He lived his faith as a servant of Christ on and off campus. His involvement with students and leadership in campus ministry gave him firsthand exposure to the challenges and struggles of living out the Christian faith as a student. In *Freshman 15* he offers biblical insights to help students not only survive, but to thrive in their faith during their student years. In fact, these principles will not only help students grow during their college years, but throughout life. I commend this book to you and pray that you will not only read it, but apply it to your life.

-Dr. Steve Crouse, Vice President for Campus Ministries, North Greenville University

Wow! What a great book! The timing is perfect because my daughter is going to college this year. I cannot wait until she reads *Freshman 15*. This book is a safeguard for upcoming college students and an inspiration to me as a speaker. I feel like Travis opened up the Scriptures and simply applied them to a college student. I loved reading it!

-Adrian Despres, Itinerant Evangelist, Vice-President Kingdom Building Ministries, FCA Chaplain for University of South Carolina Football Team

Freshman15

Freshman15

How to put the weight on in all the right places.

Travis Agnew
travisagnew.org

Tag Publishing

To Amanda

I love loving Jesus with you.

Contents

Acknowledgments

I am so grateful that the writing of this book was not an isolated effort. Many special people helped in one way or another. I would like to thank my proofreader (Joyce Fortner), my content advisors (Jeff Lethco, Phillip Howle, Chuck Lawless, Stephen Rutland, and Kelly King), my graphical genius (Cory Wilson), and my motivator encouraging me to get this book done (Amanda Agnew).

Thanks to the men of LPA for providing the majority of this content, the congregation of North Side Baptist Church for providing me a place to minister to college students, and the campuses of North Greenville University and Lander University for providing a harvest field.

I pray that Jesus gets glory from the following pages.

Introduction

Freshman fifteen is an Americanized concept proposing that when students conclude their freshman year at college, they are approximately fifteen pounds heavier than when that school year began. The theory rests on the fact that many college students experience an increase in their weight due to an excessive amount of alcohol, lack of sufficient exercise, and the consistent consumption of unhealthy food eaten at an unwise time and in exorbitant amounts.

My theory is that every college student will gain weight in college, but that doesn't have to be a negative thing. People in the ancient world spoke of giving weight to something as giving it glory or heightening it to a place of significance in one's life. You give something weight by valuing it. In your time at college, you will put on the freshmen fifteen. I would just recommend that you put it on in all the right places.

You have a choice as you enter your college experience. Where you direct your devotion is completely up to you. No parent, roommate, or professor can choose it for you. You now have an unprecedented amount of freedom to finally let you be you. So, who are you going to be?

When I entered college, I attempted to give weight to Jesus Christ in every area of my life. I was a Christian, but I arrived at an impasse of deciding if I was truly going to follow him or not. In college, I didn't have a perfect track record. I made more mistakes than successes, but with every passing experience, I realized that life was just a whole lot better when I desired Jesus to get involved in every area.

In my first job out of college, I worked with college students every day who had to make the same decision. I saw students struggle in relationships, calling, obedience, and finding God's will. In every one of those areas, each college student would decide whether or not he or she would give Jesus glory through the decision. Would the student decide to take Jesus' teachings seriously? Would the student desire to date according to biblical principles? Would that student resolve to take Christ at his word and try something impossible on his or her campus?

The following fifteen chapters are my attempt at helping you live life in college the way Christ intended. You won't find a lot of opinions in the following pages. When I entered college, I received many devotional books geared towards college students that were fluffy and unable to address my genuine struggles. I desired Jesus' word on my situations and nobody's clever opinions.

So, that's what you will find. In my experience, fifteen crucial areas exist in a college student's life that if he or she does not give weight to Jesus in, things just get messy. You can read this book straight through, or you can read these chapters independently. Read it with a friend or a small group Bible study. However you read this book, attempt to read the biblical passages referenced. If you biblically address these fifteen areas with the wisdom of Scriptures, I truly believe that you will not merely survive college as a Christian, but you will thrive as one.

If you're going to put on the weight somewhere, why not start here?

the **One Thing**

Whatever it is, it had better be worth it.

When I browse through eBay, I often wonder how I shopped before this innovative website came into existence. Before eBay, where could I find a Mr. T. t-shirt with the words, "I Pity the Fool" plastered across the front just a couple of clicks away from the original Duck Hunt version on the 8-bit Nintendo? Only here can one find the finer things of life.

Currently, this company has an advertising slogan that says, "Whatever it is, you can find it on eBay." It's probably true. Whatever the "it" is in your life that you could be possibly be looking for, this site is the best possible place to find it.

Just like we all have an "it" that we want to buy, we all have an "it" for which we are living our lives. It might be a person that you just can't get out of your mind. Maybe it is the ever-elusive American Dream. Approval may be the one thing that you spend your whole life pursuing. You might desire to make a significant impact on the world before you die. We all have our specific "it."

Whatever "it" is, "it" had better be worth it. Because if you spend your whole life pursuing it, the value of your pursuit had better be worth the price of the only life you've got to spend.

Your college life will be strikingly similar to eBay. Whatever it is, you can find it in college. If you are looking for unadulterated freedom from your parents in college, look no further. If you are searching for a party that starts your freshman year and will not stop until you graduate (four, five, or six years later), look no more. If you desire to find the love of your life one week and find another love of your life the following week because your first love of your life turned out to be a tad too clingy with a touch of unstable tendencies, the dating options for you will be plentiful. If your heart's desire is to graduate with honors, you can do it with just the right amount of cramming and lack of sleep. Whatever it is, you can find it in college. But whatever it is, it had better be worth it.

Just take a trip into your school cafeteria and you will see the division of people separated by the ambition that drives them. You will see a table of jocks brimming with testosterone. Each individual player's one thing is to be the greatest student athlete who sets the school record and gets drafted in order to get paid tons of money to play a sport he would gladly play for free.

Then there's the table with the computer geeks. They commit identity theft simply because they can. They can hack into any account. They can write any program. It's hard for them to carry on an intelligent conversation because they can't type it to the other person. The ambition at this table might be to get a well-paying job developing websites or video games.

A good many tables over, you find the sorority girls. They are wearing matching shirts and carrying the same line of bags. Their hairstyles are strikingly similar to one another. They not only look alike, but they talk alike. Each girl's ambition is to be the most popular girl on campus, and with the right amount of behavior and exposure, she could easily succeed at that goal.

Whatever it is, you can find it in college. And whatever it is, it had better be worth it because you only have one shot at college. You also only have one shot at life, so how are you going to spend your one life?

I entered college unsure of my answer. I eagerly anticipated a fast-paced college experience filled with doing whatever my heart desired. Serving in many different organizations in high school, I also desired to be a leader known on my college campus. For the first time in my academic career, I actually wanted to succeed in my classes because I understood my performance would dramatically affect my job opportunities after I graduated. I also was hoping that by the time I graduated, I would be dating a girl that could stand me long enough in order to marry me some time in the near future.

However, I also entered into college as a Christian. I committed to follow Jesus when I was seven years old. The following eleven years were full of advances and setbacks, but I was entering college still desiring to love Jesus better. The problem was that if I chose Jesus to be my one thing, the "it" for which I was going to live, he was going to affect all that other stuff.

I knew I couldn't live for a few of those things. It would be impossible. I had to choose. But whatever I decided to make my one thing, everything else in my college experience was going to have to submit to that priority.

 I learned about the need to make a decision concerning the one thing even before classes started my freshman year. Recently, more colleges have chosen to bring in the freshman class a week before classes begin to indoctrinate them to the systems of campus life. Most freshmen feel as if they are at summer camp. Some programs divide the students into random groups hoping they will bond with one another through icebreakers, ropes courses, and other random activities. Freshmen have to attend seminars on how to check out books in the library, make an identification card, wash laundry, and tie shoes and such.

As many freshmen do, I slipped away towards the end of the week from attending all the activities. I was actually looking forward to classes beginning so I would have something to do! On the Friday before classes began, I borrowed my roommate's bicycle to take a nice afternoon stroll through a nearby golf course. Not until the golfers began to tell me I was number one with their middle finger did I realize that bike riding was frowned upon on this elite golf course. As the expletives began to resonate within my ears and the golf balls began to whiz past by my head at an impressive velocity, I decided to stroll back to the main road.

As I approached the highway at an increasingly fast speed, I heard an eerie clicking noise underneath me. The bike came to a screeching halt. My body flew over the handlebars at the speed formerly held by the bike. As I slid across the concrete onto the highway, I decided to find a new hobby.

After the mile hike of limping alongside a bike with a broken chain, I finally arrived back at the dorm. When my sweet roommate saw my bloodied condition, his thoughtful words emerged gracefully from his mouth as he asked, "What did you do to my bike?"

Our freshman year was starting out just right. As soon as I got into my dorm room, I tragically realized that my watch was missing. This watch was special. My girlfriend at the time (soon to be my wife) had given that watch to me as a graduation present with an inscription on the back. Attempts at finding it were unsuccessful, and for the first time since we started dating, I dreaded seeing her that weekend. Don't get me wrong, I wanted to see her, but I was afraid of having to face someone I loved and tell her I had lost the gift she had given me.

That encounter made me think of another possible dreadful situation. Imagine having to face God and tell him that you lost the precious gift of life that he gave you. Imagine reaching heaven and encountering Jesus and admitting to him that while you made the wise decision of becoming a Christian to ensure entrance into heaven, you never really did anything beyond that decision. You went to church occasionally. You helped out someone in need when you felt really guilty. You obeyed the easier commandments, but you never really went after it. I feared saying, "Jesus, thank you for the gift of that life on your world, but to be honest with you, I truly lost it. I wasted my life, and I will never be able to get it back."

There has never been a better time in your life to decide to make Jesus your one thing. Since everyone is going to live for one thing, shouldn't you decide to live for the one thing that gave you that life? Why not make the commitment that your life is going to be characterized by the one who gave it to you? If you want your life to count, then deciding to follow Jesus exclusively in college is your best shot.

> Since everyone is going to live for one thing, shouldn't you decide to live for the one thing that gave you that life?

In college, you are removed from your parental influence. You don't have to go to church anymore. You don't have to be good because you are afraid your parents might find out. You can decide to follow Jesus because that's what you sincerely desire. It's one thing to obey Jesus because you feel guilty. Jesus' heart is that you follow him and obey his commandments and that those commandments are not a burden to keep (1 John 5:3), but they are actually a delight to keep (Psalm 119:35).

One Ambition

After graduating college, I served as college pastor to my home church. As we began to develop a strategy for college ministry, God used a specific passage of Scripture to impact my life and to guide the direction of our church's emphasis. In 2 Corinthians 5, the Apostle Paul is trying to help this church at Corinth understand the difference between the temporal and the eternal. He is trying to educate them that they will not live forever on this earth. They will live forever but not in their current location and not in their current state. He is also attempting to teach them that how they live in this life has significant impact on the life hereafter.

As we live on this earth, as you live on your college campus, we always need to be mindful that our present reality isn't it. There is more to life than our tiny perspective as we see it in the here and now. Above anyone else, Christians ought to long to live for things of eternal weight rather than temporal insignificance (2 Cor. 5:2). While we are on this earth, we are to remain faithful to Jesus (2 Cor. 5:6-8).

After that verse, Paul teaches this incredible statement in verse nine: "So whether we are at home or away, we make it our aim to please him." Did you catch that? Whether we are at home (heaven) or away from home (earth), our goal is to please him. What is our driving force in life? What is our ambition? What is the obsession for which we wake up in the morning? What's the lingering thought that keeps us up at night? Our ambition is to please Jesus. He is our one thing. Above any costly treasure or tempting pursuit, our goal is that in every area of our lives we can bring Jesus Christ glory.

Paul follows up that thought with the reason that we are to have that one ambition: we make Jesus our one thing because he made us *his* one thing. Paul stated, "The love of Christ controls us, because we have concluded this: that one has died for all, therefore all have died; and he died for all, that those who live might no longer live for themselves but for him who for their sake died and was raised" (2 Cor. 5:14-15).

I love the fact that Paul states that Christ's love controls us. It is not Christ's commands, though that should be enough. It is not Christ's power as he beats us into submission. When we truly grasp the love of a sacrificial Savior who would die in our deserving place, that love controls us. We cannot be the same. If we truly grasp the deep love which Christ has for us (1 John 3:1), that understanding compels us to live accordingly.

We no longer desire to live for ourselves. We want to please him. If my sins were punishable by death (Rom. 6:23) and someone took that punishment upon himself (Rom. 5:8), then I should be so compelled by love that I want to please him with everything I have.

Doggie Boxes As a college student, you will begin to understand the necessity of the Waffle House in your life. When you have procrastinated studying so long that you must find refuge in a place open at three o'clock in the morning, you normally end up at the Waffle House. For whatever reason, the smell of scrambled eggs with a side of prolific cigarette smoke helps the mind focus for a long night of studying.

I would normally order the newest breakfast special when I ate there. No matter what was on the plate, I normally would stir it into a makeshift pile of breakfast casserole. For some reason, it always seemed better to me when I combined it that way.

Some of you are grossed out at the idea. I understand you completely. You are a food isolationist. You can't stand the thought of eating a meal where the food is touching. If the green bean juice creeps over to the macaroni and cheese, you might as well call it a night. Even when people show you anatomy diagrams of how the food all ends up in the same place, you can't stand the thought of eating that way.

I can empathize with you. I am a recovering food isolationist, but over time, I came to endure when my food touched. In some cases, I even liked it. I didn't even require one of those doggie boxes that had the separate compartments.

Many college students treat their spiritual life like a compartmentalized doggie box. You have your relationships in this big section. In the side section, you have your college major. Your leisure time is in another compartment. You finish off your box with a side of Jesus, and life as you know it is great.

Its great as long as everything stays in its proper place. You probably are aware of Jesus' reputation that he likes to try to move into other sections, but you are making your best attempts at keeping him at bay. You love Jesus. When you need Jesus, you call on him. In reality, he is a part of your life, and you don't intend him to be anymore than that.

There's just one problem: Christ was never meant to be a part of your life. He *is* your life (Col. 3:4). He desires to take every compartment of your life and mix it together into one gigantic casserole where he has reign over every area. If you truly desire him to be your one thing in college, you give him complete freedom to do as he wishes in your life. Your time, relationships, school work, activities, date life, religious activities, and everything else you can think of comes under his influence.

As social networking sites have transitioned from a fun outlet into the current cultural phenomenon of community, I have learned more and more about collegiate Christianity. In college students' profiles, I am overwhelmed with the conflicting messages. So many college students post how important Christ is in their lives. Statements like "Jesus is everything" or "I'm nothing without God" or "faith is the most important thing in my life" are seen so much they almost lose their meaning. They truly lose their meaning when other areas of a student's profile celebrates promiscuous sex, irresponsible nightlife activities, or blatant rejections of God's standards. Students desiring hell insurance apart from expected obedience fill the halls of every college.

> **Christ was never meant to be a part of your life. He *is* your life.**

A few years ago, I knew a lady who uttered the words I think many college students inwardly feel. When discussing the expectations of a disciple of Jesus, this person stated, "Whatever happened to just being saved?" By this statement, she tried to justify her carefree behavior and negligence of obedience to Christ. Whatever happened to saying a prayer, getting a promise of eternity in heaven, and then just living however you wanted for the rest of your life?

Many college students desire to have the benefits of Jesus without the commitment to Jesus. If Jesus is your one thing, you have to begin to surrender every area in your life to him.

The Restraints

If you decide that you want to make Jesus your one thing in college, you are going to face some obstacles. In fact, you are going to have distractions come at you from every angle trying to veer you off course. While the distractions come in many forms, normally they appear in the following categories:

Unhealthy Relationships. I never understood why my mom made such a big deal about my friends when I was growing up. But as I entered college, I noticed something about all college students: the quality of the people around them determined their own quality. From the people you hang out with, to those you live with, to those you date, these relationships will do more to form you spiritually than you can possibly imagine.

Unclear Boundaries. College students who don't merely survive in college but thrive in college are students who established boundaries in critical areas. They resolved to be intentional concerning how they spent money. They were careful about what they allowed to impact them and shape their minds. They didn't cut themselves off from the world, but they did get practical concerning boundaries. For if you don't set up clear moral boundaries, you will go too far every time.

Unintentional Development. Past praying a prayer with a minister, most college students don't intentionally nurture their relationship with Christ. By neglecting spiritual development, students not only find their walk not progressing, but they actually back away from convictions they once had. Growth doesn't happen by accident. If you want to make Christ your one thing, you had better make sure that you don't fall prey to assuming you will grow spiritually devoid of any intentionality.

Potential vs. Kinetic

The next time you have a bottled soft drink, I encourage you to try a scientific experiment that shows the difference between potential energy and kinetic energy. Take the bottle full of a carbonated beverage, shake it up for a very long time (put it in the washer, drag it behind your car, throw it down the stairs, etc.). If you look closely, you will see potential energy displayed within that rumbling bottle. The fizz that is displayed through that clear container is telling you one thing: open the lid on this bottle and get sprayed in the face. If that lid is never removed, the drink will always remain as potential energy.

If you dare to remove the lid, you will experience the power of kinetic energy all over your face and all over your dorm room. The potential energy has turned into kinetic energy and the results are obvious.

The same is true for you. Most collegiate Christians are like a bottle full of potential energy. God has given them so many passions, abilities, and opportunities to do so much for the Kingdom when they are in college. The problem is that they never tap into it. God has stirred them up on the inside to do great and mighty things, but they never allow that to happen. They stay bottled up and struggle with the tension of living for Christ on a godless campus all their years in college.

I have a buddy who is the poster child for that type of living. Josh truly loves Jesus. He got saved in high school and really saw God do some amazing things in his life. Even though he messed up a bunch after becoming a Christian and struggled with certain areas of obedience, he was growing. When he got to college, he was at the best place of his life to grow. He had the foundation, the skills, and the people around him to help, but he got sidetracked.

He actually got sidetracked quite often. His rededication cycle was more frequent that his changing of majors (and that is saying a lot). He lived for other "its." He sought happiness in girls, sports, fraternity parties, and everything else college had to offer. About every six months, his pursuits would lead him to another dead end; he would feel convicted, seek counsel, rededicate his life to Christ, progress for a few weeks, and then he would start the cycle again with some moral lapse on his part.

His story is a lot like the story of Solomon. He enjoyed every type of pleasure the world had to offer and found out that it led nowhere (Ecc. 3:9-11). At the end of his experiment in attempting to find satisfaction, Solomon eventually stated that the whole duty of man should be summed up by fearing God and keeping his commandments (Ecc. 12:13).

I tried to tell Josh that fact over and over. If he could only grasp that to make Christ his one thing in life is not limiting him. It is not taking away his fun. If anything, making Jesus your one thing in college is the only way to truly experience the abundant life God promised (John 10:10). He has such potential energy, but he has never truly learned how to harness all that God wants to do and watch God at work within him.

Freshman 15 is an attempt to help you make the most out of college. The following fourteen principles won't work apart from this one. If you truly believe that you have been ransomed by Jesus Christ, you must resolve to make him your one thing. When questions about relationships or jobs or majors or morality come up, everything gets filtered through this first step. You must decide to put on weight here. If you truly want to live for Christ in college, you must decide to make Jesus your one thing. If you get that down, everything else becomes very simple.

Second Chances

Remember my watch that I lost? Amazingly, the Friday when I was going to visit Amanda, I received a call early that morning. As I picked up the phone, the caller identified himself as working for public safety. As I began to confess innocence to the prank that happened to their van the night before, the caller assured me that was not his purpose in calling. He was calling to tell me he had found my watch and wanted to know if I wanted to get it back. Of course, I wanted it back. It was a precious gift and I wanted to make sure I used it to the fullest.

Here's your chance. Your college experience is before you. If you are starting college, you have a great chance to start. If you have lived some years in college and already messed up, welcome to a second chance. The gift is being presented to you. Now what are you going to do with it?

Group Questions

Chapter 1: the One Thing
Whatever it is, it had better be worth it.

1. Name some of the "one things" that you see students living for on your campus.

2. What are the main areas in college students' lives in which they try to "keep Jesus out?"

3. Read 2 Corinthians 5:6-10. If you decide to make your one thing pleasing Jesus, what are some of the possible obstacles that will come your way?

4. Read 2 Corinthians 5:11-15. What would it look like to live for Christ during your college years in such a way to honor his sacrifice on the cross?

5. To truly make Jesus your one thing, what other things are you going to need to remove from your life?

Pray that you ruthlessly eliminate any other things that compete with Jesus being your one thing.

the Guidebook

The Bible will benefit you only as much as you treasure it.

When I was younger, I loved puzzles. I excelled at the puzzles that only had ten pieces, but as I got older, society imposed all these extra rules upon me. A fifteen-year-old shouldn't still be struggling with a ten-piece puzzle, so I had to progress. The more pieces you get though, the harder it becomes to complete the puzzle. We used to purchase puzzles that would cover the entire kitchen table. We would dump all the pieces out and eagerly get started. As the puzzles became more complex, I normally would find all the edge pieces, connect the perimeter together, get frustrated in my attempts to put together the middle, quit in utter despair, and play a video game to console myself.

Imagine trying to put together one of those puzzles on your own. I'm not even talking about without the help of another person. I'm talking about taking away the most pivotal element to completing a puzzle: the box top. The box top is so critical to putting together a puzzle because you have no framework to know how to start without it. You have no concept of where to begin or what the finished product is supposed to look like. Without the box top, puzzle construction would be nearly impossible.

A box top to a puzzle is a lot like a worldview. A worldview is simply how someone views the world. The way someone views everything that is considered knowable comprises a worldview. All the things that you think about God, life, and faith are individual puzzle pieces within a worldview. The reason why bad things happen to good people is a puzzle piece. The purpose for one's life is another piece. The method about finding a spouse is another piece. Without the box top, it is nearly impossible to put all these pieces together. Your worldview is your box top. It is how you attempt to put all these pieces of life together and make sense of the complexity surrounding us.

Even if you didn't realize it, you have a worldview. You may have never expressed a worldview out loud, but you still have one. I can prove it to you. Do you have opinion concerning how this world came into being? Do you possess a belief concerning what happens once you die? Do you hold certain actions to be morally wrong while upholding others as right? If you answered yes to any of those questions, you already possess a worldview.

While your worldview answers many questions, five questions serve as those outside pieces that give structure to your entire worldview. First, where did all this get started (creation)? Second, who are we (identity)? Third, what's the purpose of life (meaning)? Fourth, how are we supposed to live (morality)? Finally, where's all this heading (destiny)?

Even if you are not specific in how you answer those five questions, you do possess an opinion about all of them. Those five things comprise your worldview, but where did your worldview come from? Is it solely logic? Is it mere assumptions? Are you just holding a system of beliefs on a hunch? Or does your worldview come from some source of authority?

If you truly want to make Jesus your one thing, then the next area to give him glory in your life is through possessing a biblical worldview. To give God glory in this area, you must commit to answering those questions based upon biblical teaching rather than man's opinions.

University Exile

The Apostle Paul warned believers when he wrote, "See to it that no one takes you through hollow and deceptive philosophy, according to human tradition, according to the elemental spirits of the world, and not according to Christ" (Col. 2:8). The word "philosophy" literally means "the love of wisdom." Wisdom is not a bad thing. Hollow and deceptive obsession with wisdom is a bad thing. When you walk onto your university campus, you will be barraged with an onslaught of attempts at gaining wisdom completely devoid of God. The deceptive part about that attack is wisdom apart from the All-Wise one does not exist. We are unable to obtain wisdom apart from the giver of wisdom. The fear of the Lord is the very first step to knowledge which leads to wisdom (Prov. 1:7). Someone with true discernment will seek God's wisdom versus turning to the teachings originating from this fallen world (Prov. 17:24).

Wisdom that is comprised of the best human traditions always falls short. God's Word is sufficient. It has been tested and tried over the years, and the closer one scrutinizes the biblical claims, the more that person will find that the answers are true and reliable. The Bible does not need someone to defend it - the message defends itself.

If you attend a secular university, you will be labeled as a backwards hick if you claim to believe the message of the Bible. Compared to the state of the church around the world, the university campus should not be classified as full-scale persecution, but most campuses in this country are nothing less than hostile to a Christian worldview. If you choose to live and to think godly, you will be persecuted at some level (2 Tim. 3:12). If you are to maintain credibility in front of your professors and classmates, your worldview must be backed by more than heartfelt faith. While that faith is essential to your salvation, you must begin to think through why you believe what you believe.

I have taught religion classes at a secular university. One thing I have encouraged these students to do is to use their minds and their hearts when it comes to religion. Many of them were spoon fed religion as a child by their parents and believe what they believe based upon family tradition. Once they enter into college, they are spoon fed humanism and postmodernism by professors, and many students have not thought through the questions these professors propose. In light of these forces in their lives, many students jump from

> You must not only know what you believe. You must know why you believe what you believe.

worldview to worldview based upon who the current authority is in their lives.

A faith that is not personally possessed is not real faith. Faith by association is not genuine. I encourage students that regardless of what they believe, they need to own it. You must not only know what you believe. You must know why you believe what you believe.

Students on secular campuses find themselves in the same situation as a young man, Daniel, and his friends did years ago. His nation Israel had been captured by the idolatrous Babylon. The king of Babylon, Nebuchadnezzar, took the best and the brightest of the young adults from Israel in order to assimilate them into the Babylonian worldview (Dan. 1:3-4). The king knew this fact about a culture: if he can sway the worldviews of the best and the brightest of a nation, the rest of the people will not be far behind. Not only was the king promoting his worldview's agenda, but also he was subverting these Jewish young men from the worldview that they had come to possess internally.

This story is very similar to most college campuses. The best and the brightest are prime for mental molding, and professors with every possible worldview imaginable are eager to do the instructing. The worldview of this collegiate generation will affect the future of this world. If you believe the Bible, you must acknowledge that spiritual forces are at work on your campus. A struggle is taking place in the classrooms for the minds of each and every student (Eph. 6:12). Forces are assisting your ability to maintain a biblical worldview, but opposing forces are also retaliating by attempting to infiltrate your belief system.

How did Daniel and his friends respond? They resolved that they would not be defiled by the king's provisions (Dan. 1:8). He stepped out on faith. He decided that even in a idolatrous culture, he was going to remain unmoved. In the midst of a pagan society, he was going to remain faithful to God. No matter what temptations or obstacles would come his way, he decided to remain steadfast to God's commands.

If you are a Christian studying on a college campus, you will have to resolve to do the same things. You will have to prepare to meet challenges as you express a biblical worldview. In your attempt to remain untainted by the ideologies of the world, you will have to commit to allowing God to shape your mind and thinking. You must commit to an authoritative source.

Absolutely No Absolute Truth

In a time of postmodern thinking, authorities are n o t p o p u l a r. Postmodernism is the prevalent worldview that states there is no absolute truth. When someone tells me there is no absolute truth, I normally reply, "Are you absolutely sure?" That statement is an absolute statement claiming that no statement can be absolute. It is a self-defeating statement. It is false by its own standards.

"It's true for you but not for me." Can I also say the same thing about that previous statement? Postmodernism, while it is the current cultural trend, does not hold water. The rebellion against authority has caused many minds to attempt to remove God. If someone can remove the God factor out of society, that person has just now replaced God. Christianity's claims concerning a Creator God who has commands for people to live by unnerve our culture, and they try to find a way out.

The problem with postmodern thinking is the rejection of the concept of truth. Postmodernism espouses that every way towards God is an acceptable approach. If all religions lead to God, how can someone explain the contradictory faith statements? Hindus claim that the universe is eternal, but Jews claim the universe had a beginning. Both cannot be correct. Christians claim Jesus rose from the dead; Muslims claim that he never died. Those statements are irreconcilable. While our culture demands religious tolerance, these religions' beliefs make that ideal an impossibility. There is a difference in being religiously tolerant and passively agreeable. You *do* have the right to think your beliefs are correct in relation to someone else's beliefs. You do not have the right to be a jerk about it, but no one can tell you that you can't believe what you believe. That's part of the postmodern credo.

While truth may be difficult to acquire, that does not make it impossible. If we leave the quest for truth in our culture to human opinions, we will never obtain resolution. If we are to know truth, we must submit to some authority that is above all people. As a Christian, it is pivotal that you accept Christ as that authoritative figure in your life. Most college students I know are closet syncretists. Syncretism is the act of combining religious beliefs and practices and making something brand new. It's a worldview casserole. Many collegiate Christians accept certain elements of biblical teaching, but they sprinkle in postmodern thinking, pop culture's opinions, and tolerant religious teachings. With this combination, they come out believing something very alien from the gospel of Jesus. The level at which you do not submit to the truth of the gospel is the level at which you will be assimilated into your culture's worldview. If you are going to survive this battle for truth, you must go to an authority higher than yourself. To obtain a godly worldview, you must rely on God's gift: the Bible.

5 Types of Bibles

To truly let God shape your worldview, you must not only filter the teachings of your culture in order not to be conformed, but also you must be transformed by the renewing of your mind as you study the Word of God (Rom. 12:2). In God's sovereignty, he inspired human authors to write the pertinent information concerning life, faith, the world, and most importantly, himself.

The Bible was composed by forty different authors who served in every position and level of society. These authors lived in thirteen different countries. The writings came from three different continents. The Bible's contents were written down in three different languages over a time period of 1,500 years or forty generations worth. The sixty-six books that make up the Bible contain 1,189 chapters, 31,173 verses, and 783,137 words all amazingly displaying a unifying message. The Bible is all about God and his plan to redeem a fallen people.

The Bible is the box top for a Christian's worldview. In its pages, God reveals answers to the questions that mankind is asking. In the pages of Scripture, you can find how the world was created, the purpose for life, the manner in which we should live, the description of the afterlife, and so much more. The Bible is a treasure of answers for the Christian desiring to comprise a worldview according to God's standards.

While the Bible is a treasure, it will only benefit you as much as *you* treasure it. In a world that attempts to ignore biblical teaching, you must realize that the Bible will benefit you only as much as you treasure it. In my time as a college student and working with college students, I have come to realize that five types of Bibles are very prevalent on campuses.

The Tattered Bible. The Tattered Bible is a rare commodity. This worn out book is not in its current state due to neglect or abuse. The owner of this Bible has not taken it for granted or failed to protect it. The owner actually loves God so much that he or she cannot get enough of it. The wear and tear of this Bible is due to the owner's intense passion to know the Word.

If you open it up, you will see passages underlined in Habakkuk just as much as you would see in James. The pages are imprinted with the fingerprints of a Christian who knew that in order to love God better, that person would need to know God better. In order to know God better, he or she decided to read God's Word intentionally. This person not only hears the Word, but also does the Word (James 1:22). This person puts the Word into practice. When complications arise, this person goes to the Tattered Bible to inquire of God's Word rather than mere man's opinions. The owner of the Tattered Bible loves God and wants to grow more like him.

The Study Bible. The second type of Bible is the Study Bible. This massive conglomeration of pages sandwiched between two pieces of genuine leather is dressed to impress. It weighs a lot. It is bulletproof. It has Scratch-n-Sniff portions in order to experience the author's culture better. The owner of this Bible is a serious student of the Word.

The problem is that the owner is not a serious applier of the Word. The owner has read the Bible a bunch and knows all the key stories and verses. But for all the knowledge the owner possess, it never translates into life transformation. The owner possesses a lot of information devoid of application. Reading the Bible has turned legalistic and not heartfelt.

The Suffocated Bible. The third type of Bible is the Suffocated Bible. This Bible can't breathe because the owner's life is choking the air out of it. The fast pace at which this owner is living keeps him or her from ever getting deep into its pages.   This owner loves God but lacks discipline to make scriptural intake a priority.

If the owner is a college student, he or she is so determined to please other people and organizations on campus that the only person he or she says no to is God. Since God is the most forgiving person in this owner's life, the relationship with God always takes the back seat. This owner would never dream of disappointing other people, but by neglecting God's Word, the owner is not disappointing God but actually hurting himself (James 1:24).

The Emergency Bible. The fourth type of Bible is the Emergency Bible. This owner cracks open the Emergency Bible in times of crises just like a first aid kit. When tragedy strikes, when questions arise, and when doubts emerge, this owner runs to the Emergency Bible for a quick fix. Once this person makes it through the crisis, the owner promptly returns the Emergency Bible to standby mode just in cause another tragedy comes in the owner's direction.

Have you ever had one of those friends who only came around when he or she needed something? Normally, you dislike that type of friend. You tend to resent his or her presence due to the fair-weather friend status. The owner of the Emergency Bible is like that with God. The owner only fosters that relationship when he or she needs something.

The Dusty Bible. The final type of Bible is the Dusty Bible. This Bible is dusty because it is simply never used. The owner thinks the biblical message is irrelevant, impractical, and incorrect. This Bible is acknowledged as sacred perhaps, but it carries no weight in the mind of its owner.

The owner of this Bible will often claim that the Bible is too complex of a document to comprehend. By mentioning the challenges accompanying becoming a student of the Bible, this owner excuses the need to study its message. Most of us don't let a challenge slow us down from something we truly desire. If you get an electronic gadget for Christmas that is hard to use, you don't keep it in the box due to frustration with its confusing mechanical nature. If you want to use it, you work at it. The owner of the Dusty Bible is at that crossroads. If the owner truly wants to know God's Word, he will figure it out. Until then, he will continue to miss out on God's answers to the world's questions.

The Change

I entered into college with the Dusty Bible. Raised in church, I was very familiar with biblical concepts. I had an ability to retain important info concerning key biblical narratives. I knew just enough to make me dangerously complacent.

When I felt conviction about understanding God's Word, I often had people make me feel guilty about not spending time with God. A minister would pitch the idea that God is waiting in heaven for his kids to come spend time with him, and we didn't need to leave him hanging. This pitiful concept of a lonely God did not motivate me. It brought me guilt, but it never motivated me to change.

I changed the day my theology got straight. One day I realized that when I neglected time in God's Word, God wasn't the one missing out. I was the one missing out. My complacent attitude towards the intake of God's Word led me to the mediocre life I was living. The fact that I wasn't reading the Bible did not make God lonely or unable to run the universe, but I was sincerely missing out on getting closer to him. Make no mistake, if you are ignoring God's Word, he is not the one missing out. You are passing by the richest of blessings this life has to offer.

When I was in middle school, I played on the offensive line for our school's football team. I lined up next to a guy who always forgot the play that had been called by the time we made it to the line of scrimmage. His ADD kept him daydreaming in the huddle, and he would have to ask me on the line what he was supposed to do. When you are lined up against defenders, its hard to guard secrecy from the other team when you have to point in a direction for your teammate to block. Unfortunately, I had no choice. If he didn't get the play right, somebody got hurt. His lack of focus on the play led to someone on our team taking a hit.

My lack of biblical intake was causing serious setback. When I missed out from getting the play called daily from God's Word, I was not the only one suffering. As I neglected God's Word, those around me were suffering. Without God's Word resonating within my spirit, I was not changing for the better. I was lacking a genuine message telling me how I needed to change.

Then one day, I finally got sick of it. I got tired of being ungodly. I was worried that conviction was rarely present in my life. I was sick and tired of playing the Bible guessing game as I tried to hone in on a scriptural passage that I should have known the location of by that time in my Christian journey. I knew little of the Bible, and therefore, the Bible was having little impact upon me. One day in college, enough was enough.

I started reading. I underlined phrases that impacted me. I sought out answers for the questions confronting me during devotional times. Concerning those verses that purely devastated me, I put them on a list of verses I intended to memorize. The more I read, the more I wanted to know. The more I knew about the Bible, the more I loved Jesus. The more I studied his words, the more sure I become concerning those questions that comprise a worldview. The Bible began to benefit me immensely because I began to treasure it completely.

> I knew little of the Bible, and therefore, the Bible was having little impact upon me.

I read the Bible cover to cover for the first time in my life when I was in college. Through its teachings, I became confident concerning the origin of the world. God created it out of nothing (Gen. 1:1). Everything was made by him and for him (Col. 1:16). My identity was wrapped up in him. While I was made in his image, I rebelled against his standard, and therefore sin has corrupted me and the entire world (Rom. 6:23). Through Christ, my identity changed into a child of God (Eph. 2:8-10). I discovered that my purpose is simply to give Jesus glory in every possible way (Acts 20:24). The call to morality was displayed in Jesus' teachings to love God and to love others (Matt. 22:37-39). If I could follow those two commands, every moral decision would be solved (Rom. 13:9). And through the pages of Scripture, I read of my blessed destiny (Rev. 21:3-4) which was decided once Jesus changed me and gave me a new life (2 Cor. 5:17). My eternity is as secure as the hands that hold it (John 10:28).

As I read its pages, it not only transformed my mind and provided me a biblical worldview, but it also transformed my life. The amazing thing about Scripture is its ability to transform rather than merely inform (Heb. 4:12). As I continued to delve into the pages of Scripture, the more I realized I was becoming like Christ. I loved the things he loved. I hated the things he stated were out of bounds. I wasn't perfect, and I didn't turn into some super-spiritual figure, but Jesus was systematically chipping away at the ugly things in my life through the power of his Word.

Where to Start   If your desire is to make obedience to Jesus your sole ambition, you must begin to construct a biblical worldview. You will not develop it by accident, and forces are intentionally working against your developing a worldview apart from the notion of God. If you desire to do more than survive in college unscathed, you will have to commit yourself to the discipline of regular biblical intake.

Even if your class load is overwhelming and you are not the most eager reader, you must decide to treasure God's Word. I began to make it a habit to read God's Word in the morning. Next to my bed, I attached a notecard to my Scooby-Doo alarm clock. On the notecard, I wrote down a lyric from the old Keith Green song, "Asleep in the Light." Every morning as I was tempted to hit snooze, I read these lines: "Jesus rose from the dead, and you can't even get out of bed." It didn't work every morning, but it normally gave me the needed jolt to get going. If I missed it because I was going to be late to class due to my chronic snooze button contact, I found time that day to spend some time in God's Word letting the Holy Spirit instruct me concerning how to live.

I found friends who were also serious about being shaped by God's Word. We kept each other accountable. We had biblical books we attempted to read during a week and checked up on each other periodically to encourage one another. I got a key ring with some note cards and began to memorize Scripture as much as I could.

If you are serious about constructing a biblical worldview, you must accompany your great intentions with some practical insurance that you get it done. The more you read Scripture, God will shape your worldview and transform your life. The key to the next steps in this journey is the Bible. All of the following concepts stem from God's truths. Without his Word, we are subject to human opinions. If you truly desire to put on the weight in this endeavor, you must remember that the Bible will benefit you only as much as you treasure it.

Group Questions
Chapter 2: the Worldview
The Bible will benefit you only as much as you treasure it.

1. From what places do most students on your campus obtain their worldview?

2. What do you believe? How would you give an answer to the issue of creation, identity, meaning, morality, and destiny?

3. In giving those answers, why do you believe what you believe? What has caused you to believe the way that you do?

4. Out of the five types of Bibles presented (tattered, study, suffocated, emergency, and dusty), which Bible would you say that you have right now?

5. Read 2 Timothy 3:12-17. The Bible must be the key to developing your worldview. What will be your plan to start regularly studying God's Word?

Pray that you begin to treasure the Bible and begin to allow its teachings to change the way you live.

the **Entourage**

Those closest to me must be closest to God.

His name was Spanky. Spartacus was his real name – Spartacus "Spanky" the Shark. He was tough, real tough. I bought him at Wal-Mart since that is where all ferocious aquatic animals are purchased. He intensely intimidated all who came into contact with him at a whopping three inches long. Spanky was a pretty tough fish.

Unfortunately, Spanky never grew much larger then when I originally purchased him. In fact, he will never grow more than what his environment lets him grow. An interesting fact about sharks is that a shark will only grow according to the size of the environment in which it is placed.

If I keep Spanky in a tiny glass aquarium all of his life, he will never be able to outgrow his restrictive surroundings. He will always be a small fish in a small bowl. If I were to take him and drop him out into the Atlantic Ocean, he would grow to a length that he could never be restrained in his glass prison because a shark will always grow according to the size of his environment.

You're just the same. Your spiritual life will only grow according to the size of the environment in which you place yourself. You will never outgrow your surroundings. If you surround yourself with people who make Jesus their one thing and get their worldview from the Bible, you will end up doing the same. If you place yourself in an environment where Jesus is not treasured, you will quickly move away from that ideal.

I always knew that intentionally placing oneself in positive environments affected one's spiritual condition, but I never realized how pivotal it was until I worked with students on a college campus. A few years ago, some staff members from my church and I were passing out promotional bags for our church at the local college's business fair. It was a typical South Carolinian August day – unbearably hot and dreadfully humid. As we passed out info and invited students to visit our church, I became increasingly devastated. By the minute, I became more and more overwhelmed at what I was experiencing. My devastation was no longer due to the heat, but it was due to the amount of students that I actually knew the names of on that campus.

Students would walk by and tell me hello and ask what was new at the church. I would recognize certain students and was able to remember their names, and ask them how their class load was going. What alarmed me was that I knew so many of the students and at some time those students had come to our church or attended one of our Bible studies, but they were no longer active in anything remotely religious. I knew how they were living, and it was not according to what they once said they believed.

They were involved at one time, but now so many of them were missing in action. I attempted to discover why they were no longer involved. Were my communication skills lacking so much that it kept them away from our Bible study? Was our church too outdated for them to perceive the message as relevant to their lives? Were we completely missing the way to minister to their needs while they were in college?

Finally, I realized a common denominator between every single student I encountered that at one time had been active but now was not growing in Christ – they had chosen bad friends.

Seems too simple of an answer? I thought so too. I kept arguing in my own mind. Surely the simple answer of having chosen bad friends is not the problem of these students. Without a doubt, every student who had at one time followed Jesus but had drifted away had surrounded himself with friends that had led him astray. I counted numerous Christians enamored with good intentions to grow but never positively enhanced their spiritual condition. They were never able to grow because the environment in which they placed themselves was not conducive for spiritual growth. These environments were actually counterproductive to their spiritual health. They never grew beyond their environment.

I then looked to the other extreme. I started listing the ten students who possessed the most contagious faith. I studied the students who were growing to be like Christ, keeping their integrity intact, and reaching out to those far away from God. They too had a common denominator – they chose great, godly friends. They differed in being blessed with godly parents. They ranged in their length of time as a Christian. They possessed differing levels of biblical knowledge, but they all had surrounded themselves with people who were crazy about Jesus. The most consistently growing students all had consistent people serving as their entourage. The people that they allowed to be closest to them were first and foremost people who were closest to God.

Building Consistency

I am one of the most inconsistent people you will ever meet. I will bowl great for three frames, and then I will reside in the gutter the rest of the game. That's not entirely true. I will reside in the gutter of the lane next to me for the rest of the game. At New Years, I will begin a steady diet and exercise routine that lasts all of twenty minutes into the New Year. I will start a span of regularly responding to emails, and then I will have a setback and not reply to anyone for six weeks. I crave consistency.

In my spiritual life, I am even worse. On a mission trip, I will turn into super-evangelistic boy on the field only to revert to an ashamed coward when I return home. My devotional life will get intense after a convicting sermon only to last until the guilt finally wears off. An answered prayer turns me into an intercessory advocate until I stop seeing immediate results to my prayers. I want to do better. I honestly do crave consistency.

Consistency requires intentionality. If I am not intentional about being consistent in my spiritual life, it will not happen. I used to believe that if I simply desired to grow badly enough, that desire would be sufficient to propel me into growth. Then I got to know myself better, and I realized that my best days are meager, and I need something more to keep me consistent. I need others.

In Psalm 1, the Psalmist describes a consistent follower of God. He wrote, "Blessed is the man who walks not in the counsel of the wicked, nor stands in the way of sinners, nor sits in the seat of scoffers" (Ps. 1:1). We all want to be like the blessed man. We want God to throw good stuff our way. It is interesting to know that the Psalmist explicitly shows a progression to follow for a person to remove himself from the promised blessings of God.

The first step in the progression is someone who begins to walk in the counsel of the wicked. It doesn't say that the person is necessarily wicked; the Psalmist simply claims that they are listening to the advice of people far from God. Have you personally witnessed that subtle shift? When a person seeks out advice from people who are far from God versus seeking godly counsel, he is well on his way. The relationship in which that person has chosen to indulge is clearly taking him down a specific path.

The second step down the path of dangerous relationships finds someone who is now standing in the way of sinners. This person is no longer just walking beside people who do bad things; he has slowed down completely to a stop. He doesn't merely pass them on the road anymore; he is spending long periods of time with people who knowingly sin against a Holy God.

The final step is the most dangerous of all. In this step, we find the person now sitting down in the seat of scoffers. A scoffer is one who mocks or shows no respect to a certain something. It is implied here that this scoffer is one who absolutely shows no respect to God. Our example is no longer just walking beside someone who does evil things; he is no longer standing with people who are characterized by sin; now he is comfortably sitting down with people who mock God and the biblical commands he once followed so closely. The progression is subtle yet deadly, and all steps occurred in the confines of relationships. This scenario is seen often when a Christian starts hanging out with people who don't esteem Jesus, and then they start traveling down a slippery slope.

That character is the antithesis to the blessed man spoken of in Psalm 1. The blessed man is one who delights in the law of the LORD, thinking about God's Word all day and all night (Ps. 1:2). The Psalmist even characterizes this man as similar to a "tree planted by streams of water" (Ps. 1:3). A tree will either flourish or fade depending upon its physical proximity and access to a sufficient water supply. The blessed man, the one who is faithful to God, knows that he has to be careful about who or what he allows to speak into his life. People who do not supremely value God cannot influence him, but God himself must influence this man. That's why those closest to you must be closest to God.

This natural progression happens on every college campus in the country. A freshman arrives at college with great anticipations of living for Jesus. This freshman had a high school graduation service at her church where she received a Bible, a devotional book for graduates, and was featured in a graduate recap video. During the service, her pastor challenged them to live for Jesus in college, and the majority of those graduating honestly had that desire.

Then she actually gets to college where it's hard to follow Christ. A couple of her church friends went to the same school, so she has a security blanket. Over time, she comes into contact with certain classmates who are having the time of their lives in college. As she begins to get to know some of those people, she realizes that they don't live for God, but she still likes hanging out with them, and she desperately doesn't want to be alone. All of a sudden, it moves past being acquaintances, and she starts being influenced by their worldview. She listens to their advice. She starts changing the way she thinks on certain subjects due to their influence in her life. She is walking in the counsel of the wicked.

After a while, her thinking on the necessity of church has shifted. She no longer believes it is important, for her friendships have helped change that thought. Currently, she is no longer merely attending events and aware of people breaking God's commands. She is starting to indulge as well. She thinks that a lot of what she was taught back home was outdated and unrealistic. She is now standing in the way of sinners and loving it.

Not too long into her college career, she finds herself no longer just merely sinning, but she is literally mocking God with her lifestyle. She laughs at narrow-minded goodie-two-shoe Christians. She is on the top of the world – sitting in the seat of scoffers, and she has found herself very far from Jesus.

You need to realize something – she did not intend to go down that path. No one who honestly loves Christ desires that ending, but in the context of unhealthy friendships, she found herself in a place she never intended to be – far from God. The number one reason was that she allowed the people closest to her to be people who were far from God themselves.

"Wasn't Jesus a Friend to Sinners?"

I get asked that question all the time. "Yeah, I hear what you are saying about relationships and such, but Jesus was a friend to sinners, and religious people were the ones who ridiculed him." That statement is entirely correct. Jesus was a friend to people who were very far off from God, but they were not his best friends.

Those closest to you must be those closest to God. Sure Jesus' disciples made mistakes, but they at least were attempting to live right in God's eyes. And those were the people with whom Jesus spent the majority of his time. He befriended sinners as if it was his job, but he had a core group of people sharing the same ambition as him.

Deciding to make the people closest to you be people who are closest to God doesn't change the need to reach out to others. That doesn't mean you don't have friendships with people who don't have a relationship with Jesus. That doesn't mean you don't befriend someone of a different religion. That doesn't mean that you avoid a party animal like the plague. All that means is if you want to stay close to Jesus, you can't let people who don't care about Jesus be the people who are the absolute closest to you (Prov. 2:12-15).

Remember that you also sin. You are not better than anyone; you are just wiser because you chose a relationship with Jesus. We are not to look down on anyone, but you are intentionally to befriend people for the sake of the gospel. In order to safely reach out, you must first establish those people who truly love God to be consistent in your life so that you can be consistent spiritually. Just as the author of Proverbs wrote, "Whoever walks with the wise becomes wise, but the companion of fools will suffer harm" (Prov. 13:20). To keep yourself godly, you need to surround yourself with people who have the same resolve.

Top 8 MySpace was one of the first social networking sites to come up with the concept of displaying your best friends when they provided a function of selecting your top eight friends to proclaim your closeness. Facebook and other sites also provided a method to show the world the most important people in your life. Like being high up on the chain of someone's speed dial, if you made someone's top eight list, you know that the security of B.F.F. (Best Friends Forever) was a legit possibility.

I think it is actually important for us to do this exercise as well. I want you to get something on which to write. Make a list of one through eight, and I want you to write out the names of the top eight people that you would say are your best friends. Whom do you plan on hanging out with this weekend? Once you have gotten down those names, you can move on to the next part.

On another list of eight, I want you to write out the names of your top eight spiritual advisors. If you were in spiritual or emotional crisis, whom would you call to help you in your dilemma? You must have confidence in these people that they would steer you in a godly direction. Once you have those top eight people, you can move onto the next section.

I want you to now see how many names were privileged enough to have made both lists. Eight? Seven? Six? Or is it somewhere even further down the line? If you don't have a good number of repeats on these two lists, let me warn you: trouble is already brewing. If the top eight people that you spend most of your time with are not people you would call on to get God's perspective during pivotal times in your life, you have already made unwise decisions concerning your entourage.

Oftentimes, you might have to go to the spiritual mentor list to help you get out of a jam which the hangout friends got you into in the first place. It should alarm you that the people who are around you the most could be causing you to endanger your walk. Bad company does corrupt good morals (1 Cor. 15:33), and if you currently have the closest people to you living lives far from God, compromising temptations are on their way if they haven't already arrived.

As Iron Sharpens Iron

My sophomore year at college, I lived in a dorm full of great guys. Many of those guys really loved Jesus and had a desire to grow spiritually. We had a great time together, but we also helped grow one another up in Christ. We started a dorm Bible study on Tuesday nights, and we would gather together to keep each other accountable. One of our focal verses was Prov. 27:17 which states, "As iron sharpens iron, so one man sharpens another." Our desire as brothers in Christ was to sharpen one another to be used as effective instruments for the Kingdom.

In our dorm, we understood the dynamics of sharpening iron. Frequently, someone in our dorm would get on a collector's kick, and other guys would follow suit to whatever was the newfound hobby. We went through a kayak phase. We shortly lived through a fishing phase. Surprisingly, knife collecting became one of the favored pastimes in our dorm for a semester. Many of the fellows in my dorm began buying pocketknives on eBay and developed quite the collection.

You might be thinking, "What did those guys need with pocket knives?" I asked the same question a hundred times with no suitable response presented. Knife collecting just happened to be the flavor of the month. They weren't killing their food or carving wood with their knives, they just liked carrying knives around because it made them feel tough and rugged. They loved sharpening the knives too. They never used them, but did they ever sharpen them. My roommate sharpened one knife so much, he would often comment on how sharp it was and how much damage it could do to anyone or anything in which he might come into contact. He found that reality out firsthand one day while sharpening his knife when he decided to extend the sharpening process to his left thigh. Evidence confirmed: the knife was sharp.

While we had to travel to the hospital a lot for dorm-related injuries, this particular visit to the emergency room made me really think. I realized that no matter what that knife contacted, it was either going to sharpen the knife or dull the knife. Every substance that knife would strike would either do one of those two things. If the substance was more durable than the knife, it would sharpen it, but if the substance was denser than the knife (let's say, oh I don't know – a leg), it would always dull the knife at least a little bit.

Spiritually speaking, every person in your life is either sharpening you or dulling you. I cannot think of a person in my life that is doing something in between. I have people in my life, that if I allowed to influence me, they would dull what God is doing in my life. I also have people in my life that are sharpening me by challenging me to become everything that God has intended. One Christ-follower is intended to sharpen another. God doesn't require us to live Christianity on an island; he has given us one another in order to actively sharpen.

> Spiritually speaking, every person in your life is either sharpening you or dulling you.

In our dorm, we made a commitment to sharpen one another. When we shared prayer requests, we actually prayed for one another and followed up to see how each situation was going. We challenged each other in Scripture memory. My roommate and I developed a game that we would often play called, "What You Going to Say?" We would challenge each other by giving a scenario that needed biblical attention and require the other one to bring God's perspective to the table from heart. One of us would present the problem: "Let's just say that I believe all roads lead to heaven. What you going to say?" The other person, who was trying to memorize God's Word in those areas, would attempt to display God's truths through the Scripture we had memorized. We both had gotten tired that we didn't know the Bible enough (Ps. 119:9-11), and so we decided to sharpen one another.

If someone in our dorm had said something that didn't reflect Christ (Eph. 4:29), we decided to love one another enough to speak the truth in love (Eph. 4:15) by biblically confronting one another (Matt. 18:15). We were able to have discussion concerning Christian liberty and cigar smoking (1 Cor. 6:12). We gave each other allowance to question the level of purity in our own lives (2 Tim. 2:22). We did missions together (1 Thess. 2:8). We grieved together by sharing one another's burdens (Gal. 6:2). For most of us, this spiritual incubator in our dorm was the time of the greatest growth any of us had ever experienced.

Spur One Another The author of the Book of Hebrews illustrated the need for one another greatly when he wrote, "let us consider how to stimulate one another to love and good deeds, not neglecting to meet together, as is the habit of some, but encouraging one another, and all the more as you see the day drawing near" (Heb. 10:24-25). I have often heard pastors use those verses for a call to be at church every time the doors are open. Unfortunately, even if you come to a church every time the doors are open, you don't necessarily achieve relationships like the ones described in these verses. The kind of spurring emphasized in these verses cannot come about by simply attending church; you must be committed to belonging to a group of people.

That's why I have often told college students that it is more important for them to be in a small group that meets regularly and shares life than for them to go to five large group Bible studies or worship services. Dramatic, life-changing transformation happens when we can look into one another's eyes and encourage each other to get closer to God. I love that passage because it implies that we must learn to study one another. We have to delve deep down to figure out what makes each one of us tick. The same thing it took to grow my roommate was not the same stimulus for all the other guys. I had to get to know each one of them and figure out how my time with them could be best spent in sharpening them.

If you try to be friends with everyone, it won't work (Prov. 18:24). If you allow yourself to get closer to people who don't follow God versus following God closely, you will find yourself growing further from God yourself. Jesus himself said, "You are my friends if you do what I command you" (John 15:14). Friends of Jesus are going to help other like-minded friends of Jesus to be obedient in every area of their lives.

Now that you have added the weight to your ambition and your worldview, it is essential that you decide to give God glory in the area of your friendships. He can provide you with a much easier walk through college if you choose good friends. Have friendships that emulate the friendship between David and Jonathan who could say that the "LORD will be between you and me" (1 Sam. 20:42).

Take some time to fill out a new top eight. Write down a list of eight people that you spiritually need in your life and do whatever you can to get around them regularly. Be on the lookout. People are as good as their closest friends are.

Just ensure that you start making those closest to you people who are getting closer to God. In their proximity, you might just do the same.

Group Questions

Chapter 3: the Entourage
Those closest to me must be closest to God.

1. In what areas do Christians normally reveal inconsistencies in their lives?

2. Read Psalm 1. How do you see the progression of someone getting further from Christ happen on your campus?

3. Who are your "Top 8?" Make a list of people with whom you need to be intentional about spending time.

4. How are you best "sharpened" spiritually? What type of motivation works best on you?

5. How can you intentionally surround yourself with a godly entourage to make sure you grow in college? Get practical.

Pray that the people closest to you are people who are closest to God. Ask God to reveal to you the next steps at developing your entourage.

the Date

If mission does not define the relationship,
then the relationship will define the mission.

When I was in elementary school, all of my friends and I used to play a game called "Mash" during class. You would diagram different columns into whom you would marry, what job would you have, where would you live, etc. This game had one important rule: you had to give four good options on the list and one bad option. For example, you would provide four names of people you wanted to marry, and then provide one name at the bottom of someone you did not want to marry in an individual column. You would then get a number where you would start marking out items in each column by that number until your entire life was figured out on that small piece of tablet paper.

Wouldn't it be great if it were that easy? It would be so simple if our major life decisions could be discerned through this easy process especially in the area of dating. Most people come to college and are excited about the dating possibilities. You encounter all these people that are ignorant concerning all of your previous drama. They don't know if you were in a relationship for your entire high school career. Word hasn't gotten out on campus that you're a playa who struggles with commitment issues. Maybe they don't even know that you actually didn't date at all in high school because you were too socially awkward. Whatever your case is, when you enter into college, you have this amazing chance to start anew.

51

In your first few weeks of college, it's easy to get overwhelmed at the amount of prospects and possibly the greater amount of rejects for you to date. Some of the people begin to perk your curiosity. You sit behind someone in biology that actually makes you look forward to going to class. You go to an organizational meeting and in one of the cheesy icebreakers you meet someone and you swear you hear light rock love songs playing in the airwaves around you. Or maybe it's that person that you seem to run into all the time around campus that you are attracted to but you just haven't gotten the nerve up to say, "Hey, I see you all the time, in the halls and in my dreams, and I was wondering if you are carrying any major relationship baggage with you that would scare me off from asking you out to a cheap Mexican restaurant?"

The scary thing about dating in college is that you know you must at least start thinking long-term. Even if you don't see yourself getting married right after graduation, you realize that every date in college has a heavier weight attached to it than it did in high school. To be honest, you can't be too serious about your dating decisions in college. Even if you are accident-prone when it comes to relationships, there is a good probability that if you start a dating relationship in college, it could actually lead towards marriage. Even if it doesn't lead to marriage, the issues that develop from your relationships during this time will significantly impact your relationships to come. Next to following Jesus, the most important decision in your life is whom you will marry. That decision will influence your life in ways you cannot begin to comprehend.

The dating warning in college is this: if mission does not define the relationship, then the relationship will determine the mission. When I speak of mission, I am talking about your particular purpose for why you are on this earth. Unfortunately, mission cannot be to marry a rich doctor and have two point five kids. That may be a goal, but your mission is something that transcends you. It's not something you created. Your mission is something that is given to you by God. If mission does not define the relationship, then the relationship will determine the mission.

1st Relationship in the Bible

When I do premarital counseling with a couple, I often ask them what was the first relationship in the Bible. Usually, the response is that the first relationship in the Bible was between Adam and Eve. The guy answers the question, the girl looks at him and giggles, and I am getting ready to theologically pounce all over him.

The first relationship recorded in the Bible was not between Adam and Eve. It was between Adam and God, and every following relationship must come at least second in devotion or else major problems exist. Marriage was the second recorded relationship in the Bible, and that's the way it should always be. Before there was ever marriage between a man and a woman, there was a deep, intimate relationship with Adam's Creator. Before sin came into the world, Adam and God walked with no separation between them. They experienced intimate fellowship as no man has experienced since. Before there was Eve, there was God. While Adam's relationship with Eve was the next greatest relationship, it was never intended to supplant Adam's relationship with God. The LORD Almighty was to be Adam's first love, and with that status, God has the rights to set up parameters in which all other relationships must succumb.

Before you can define what your relationship will be like with a boyfriend or girlfriend, you have to maintain clarity concerning your relationship with God. You need to be close to him. Once you are close in fellowship with God, then you are able to understand what your mission is about; then you have the rights to go and look for that special someone. God must come first, but Eve is second.

After a relationship with God, a marriage relationship is of utmost importance. It is so important that Adam and Eve's story helps us again. In the first couple of chapters in Genesis, a recurring song is displayed. During Creation, the song goes like so: 1) God wants something to be created, 2) he says let it be, 3) it happens, and 4) God says it's a good thing. The recording follows the same format with the universe, the trees, the fuzzy bears, the pretty stars, and everything in the world until he gets to his final creation. In Genesis 1, the big picture account of Creation, God says that all the creations are good.

In Genesis 2, the author lets us peer a little bit deeper into what happened at God's creation of human life. The one creation that God actually creates in his very own image presents a turn in the story. It happened like so: 1) God wanted man in his image to be created, 2) he says let it be, 3) Adam is created, and 4) God says that this creation is no good.

His exact words were, "It is not good that the man should be alone" (Gen. 2:18). Don't let your familiarity with this verse take you away from the significant impact of its implications. Genesis 2 comes in the Bible before Genesis 3. I know that because I went to seminary. The reason that fact is important is that in Genesis 3, the Fall of mankind occurs. Sin rushes into the world with the disobedience of the first couple. That means that when God said that Adam was alone, it was pre-Fall. Sin had not entered the world. God and Adam were walking side by side in the world together without anything separating them. Adam was experiencing an intimacy with God unparalleled in history.

Regardless of his condition, God still said that Adam was alone. The reality is that God has created us with a God-shaped void in our lives that only he can fill. Whenever we try to fill it with anything else, those substitutes always come up short. That's why the relationship with God must come first. The other reality is that God has created us with a person-shaped void in our lives that he chooses *not* to fill. He could, but he doesn't. He looked at Adam and could have met every single one of his needs, but he decided that life could be more enjoyable if our needs were met through a partnership with God and a spouse.

God Wants You to Stay Single

While that is a beautiful story of God's heart for marriage, another reality is that Genesis 3 did happen. Sin entered the world, and ever since, men and women just can't seem to get it right. After the Fall of mankind in the Garden of Eden, everything has changed. God's desire hasn't changed, but our relationships surely have changed. Due to the sin in our hearts, we have seen divorces, unfaithfulness, abuse, and neglect to name just a few. So in the area of relationships, God's will for you is for you simply to remain single. Think about it: so much heartache and pain comes from dating, so why wouldn't God prefer for you to stay single? Monks and nuns do it, why can't you?

I'm only halfway joking. God actually does prefer for you to stay single. He prefers for you to stay single-focused. He wants you to focus on your relationship with him, and anything else that is attached to your life has to support that relationship or else it becomes a competing system against God. From what I have read, God hasn't lost one of those battles yet. He always wins, and he has your best in mind, but he is determined for you to stay single-focused.

The Apostle Paul was never married. He was single his entire life. He had the gift of celibacy. I never asked Santa Claus for that particular gift, but I still believe that some people do have it. When he corresponded with the Corinthian church, they questioned Paul regarding whether they should be married at all. In their church, so much strife and pain had been caused because of sexual immorality and marital unfaithfulness, they questioned Paul concerning whether or not their church would be better off if they just remained as far away from sexual relationships as possible. It's a good logical argument, but I just personally don't endorse it.

Paul actually told them that it was better if they just stayed in whatever state they currently were (1 Cor. 7:20); he said it would be easier if they stayed single like he was (1 Cor. 7:7). He then stated that if someone was going to burn with lust all their lives desiring a sexual relationship, then it was better for him or her to go ahead and get married so that was never a constant nuisance (1 Cor. 7:9). Isn't Paul a romantic? His logic for love: the main reason to get married is to have sex (more on this idea in the next chapter).

Paul then laid out an argument based upon the spiritual and cultural climate of the time. "In view of the present distress," he encouraged them to remain as they were (1 Cor. 7:26). If they were married, stay married. If they were single, stay single. In Paul's time, Christians were on the run. Many Christians were being killed due to their association with Jesus, and Paul was telling these Corinthians that walking with Jesus and trying to develop a romantic relationship was going to cause some tension in their lives. If it were going to cause some tension, it would just be easier if they avoided marital relationships. If you got married and then you died for the cause of Christ, you were going to leave behind a widow and some orphans, and Paul just wanted to clarify that these relationships are not sinful, but they do complicate living for Christ in such times.

He stated that an unmarried man is concerned about the things of the Lord, but a married man is concerned about the things of the Lord *and* God now commands him to be concerned about his family as well (1 Cor. 7:32-34). He is now mandated to do both. Being married and having a family is not sinful; God created the whole process, but Paul's opinion was that if you could stay single, it would be a lot easier in order to do ministry.

As I'm finishing this book, I have been married for almost five years and I have a one-year-old son. I love being a husband and a father. It was God's idea for marriage, and he actually commanded his children to make lots of babies and fill up the earth so we can outbreed people who don't believe in God and keep our presence noticeable in the culture (I'm not exaggerating that one, but for room sake in this chapter, you will need to read the Bible on your own).

So none of those things are bad. In fact, God placed many commands in the Bible concerning the extreme devotion he commands me to have for my wife (Eph. 5:25) and the steadfast trustworthiness he calls me to provide for my children (Deut. 6:4-9). Realistically, in order to fulfill those commands of God, I don't have as much time to fulfill other commands of his. I can't go lead a Bible study on a college campus every night of the week since God commands me to take care of my family now too. Neither of them are bad, none of them are more spiritual than the other; Paul just wanted to provide a reality check for those who wanted a relationship. Once you are married,

> In dating, the will of God is that you stay single. Stay single-focused to obtain undistracted devotion to the Lord.

you have additional responsibilities on top of the preexisting responsibilities as being his ambassador (2 Cor. 5:20). In addition to sharing with the lost, serving in my church, reaching out to the needy, I am also commanded by God now to care of my family.

One of his concluding remarks really sums up his entire argument. Trying to clarify his desire for these Christians, he confesses that what he is trying to procure for them is "undistracted devotion to the Lord" (1 Cor. 7:35). In fact, that's the summation of that entire chapter. If someone would spend his or her life burning with lust because he or she was not married, then Paul urges that person to get married. Lust conflicts with undistracted devotion to the Lord. If you do get married, it is easy to get caught up in the distorted, Americanized view of marriage, and it becomes easy to succumb to not serving Jesus faithfully in your marriage or anywhere in your life. That worldliness competes with undistracted devotion to the Lord.

In dating, the will of God is that you stay single. Stay single-focused to obtain undistracted devotion to the Lord. If you can stay better focused to God by being married, then get married. If you can stay better focused to God by being single, then remain single. In any relationship, you must remember to submit that relationship under the devotion that you have for your most important relationship that you have with God.

Deciding whether or not to get married is not a matter of preference but of holiness. Your relationship decision should be based upon which setting would allow you to follow Christ more closely. The only way then you can decide to get married is if you can make a case before God that you can serve him better married than you can single.

Mr. or Mrs. Right?

Once you've done the hard work of figuring out whether or not you can follow Christ better married or not, then you must decide who you should date. Dating leads to marriage, so you want to be careful whom you date. I started dating my wife in eleventh grade of high school. I robbed the cradle because she was in tenth grade. I realize that is shocking, but what is even more shocking is that you could currently be in a relationship with the person you are going to marry. I hope someone reading this understands this reality and allows panic to takeover. Your response might be picking up your cell phone and texting the person you are currently dating to say "we r thru :(."

If you want to know whom to date, you must ask the question: who can help me serve Jesus better? It's that simple.

One of the worst events in elementary school was picking teams for kickball at recess. I have never been the greatest sportsman, so I was used to being picked near the end when the guys played football, but kickball was a different story. Everyone could play kickball. The time when the kid with two inch thick glasses and the girl in a cast got picked before me, I knew something had to be wrong with the universe. Didn't anybody notice she was on crutches? "Yeah, but do you know how far the ball will go if she actually can kick it with her cast?"

In reality, I don't blame them for their selections. When you play kickball or any sport, you want to build a team that has the best chance to win. You want the absolute best team players you can find. In dating, it should be no different. You want to put someone on your team that gives you the best possible chance to succeed in living for Jesus.

The Tempting Settlement

The number one danger for college students dating lies in the practice of settling. It normally falls out like so: A young lady attended a True Love Waits rally when she was sixteen, and during that weekend, she wrote down the characteristics of the man that she believed God desired her to marry one day. He was to be passionately following Jesus, faithfully growing, respectful of all people, and aware of how a godly guy should treat a lady. She had that ideal in her mind when she was sixteen, but the older she got, the more she came to believe that the guy of her dreams was just that. Approaching college graduation, she was unwilling to wait any longer on God's standard, and she settled. She settled for way less than a godly guy all because she refused to be lonely.

I can always tell if a college student is settling. If I ask about the guy a girl is dating and the response is, "he's a good Christian guy," I am confident we have trouble. Normally, the phrase, "a good Christian guy," means a guy who got saved when he was seven years old, but when he got into high school, he turned into a drunk, and he slept around a lot. He at least goes to church every once in a while if he is begged to go and none of his buddies are doing something more appealing on Sunday morning. This description does not classify a good Christian guy.

A good Christian guy has more good to say about him than that simple phrase. A guy following after Jesus doesn't have to be bragged on; he's already heard about. He is leading others closer to Jesus. He treats ladies with dignity and respect and not as a sexual object. He not only goes to church, but also gives of his time, money, and efforts back to the church. In a time when they are scarce, make no mistake about it, you will hear about a guy who is a growing disciple of Christ.

A good Christian girl is distinguishable far beyond some shallow phrase. She is more concerned with the beauty of her heart to the eyes of Jesus than she is the vain beauty that can be accomplished through makeup and good lighting. People seek her when hard times come because of her devotion and trust in God. She is unwavering and an example for all. She is not waiting for a man to come into her life before she can be satisfied; she is living for the Kingdom now.

Let's face it – those two people are hard to find! You may have that ideal out there of a great guy or girl that you meet, but quite honestly, you just don't see that many members of the opposite sex as living passionately for Jesus. And since all of your other friends are in serious relationships, your mom is questioning why you can't get a date, and you are nearing college graduation; you ultimately decide to settle. When you settle for less than God's best, you pay for it the rest of your life.

If you look around your church, you will find a settler without a doubt. You will find a lady who thought her beloved would start coming to church when they got married, but he never made good on his empty promises. You will find a man who had great ideas about leading a godly home, but overtime he was allured to settle for leading a respectable home within the community. They settled early in their lives, and they will pay for it the rest of their time on earth. And not only will they pay, but their children will also suffer. If you didn't have godly parents growing up, imagine all that God could have done through your life if you had a father and mother who treasured Jesus so much that they were the primary spiritual role models in your life? Unfortunately, too many people settle. They got the relationship in front of the mission, and then everything simply imploded after that frequently committed mistake.

Refusing to Settle

No one knows the danger more than Lottie Moon. If you grew up in a Baptist church, you might vaguely recognize her name because she was associated with people giving money to overseas missions and you got to purchase a RC Cola and a Moon Pie in church during the emphasis. Most Baptist kids love them some Lottie! She wanted to be a missionary. She wanted to serve Jesus, but she also wanted to get married.

She fell in love with Dr. Crawford Toy, an army chaplain. When they started their relationship, he was devoted to God and to his Word. They became engaged, but Lottie began to have some doubts concerning her fiancé. Toy began to flirt with Darwinism and the theory of evolution. He began to question biblical claims and started drifting away from living for Jesus. As a result of that wavering, she began to question whether she could truly love a man who did not supremely love God.

She broke off the engagement and focused solely on missions in China. It wasn't easy for her. She suffered with bouts of loneliness. She truly wanted to be married, and she deeply loved Toy. Later in her life, she was asked if she had ever truly been in love. Lottie admitted that she was definitely in love, but since God had first claim on her life, she had no real option to whom her allegiance would lie.

She spent the rest of her life on the mission field single and single-focused. She eventually did leave China. It wasn't because she got married or lonely. Her fellow missionaries made her get on a boat to receive medical attention. During that time, China had been stricken with famine and disease. Many of the people to whom she was ministering were literally starving to death. She appealed for more finances from churches back home. When she did not receive the adequate financial support, she took matters into her own hands. She stopped eating. She took the food she could have been eating and gave it to others who were starving. Eventually, she only weighed fifty pounds due to her sacrifice. The missionaries finally realized what was going on and sent her for help. She died en route in December of 1912, having never been married and leaving not a single regret.

I know what you are thinking: "I thought this chapter was supposed to be about dating?" It is, but I cannot reiterate to you enough that if mission does not define the relationship, then relationship will define the mission. If Lottie Moon had decided to allow her love interest to dictate what she did for God, millions have people would have suffered. Her life has been a catalyst for missionary efforts. If she had chosen to settle, literally millions of people would have been affected. She would have never died due to malnutrition. She would have had better living conditions. She could have experienced motherhood, stability, and affluence, but she wouldn't have been able to look Jesus in the eye in quite the same way. She chose not to settle. She remained single-focused, and Jesus was proud of her for it.

The Game Plan If you have determined that you think you can serve Jesus better through being married than being single, some practical steps do exist. First, grow in your relationship with Christ. Seek first his kingdom and his righteousness, and everything else will fall into place (Matt. 6:33).

Second, do not see this period as a waiting room for a better stage in life. Do not wait to serve Christ once you get married. Because you are single, you currently have more time to devote to the Kingdom than any other time in your life. Go serve in a country you can't spell this summer. Invest your life every week with students who need a positive role model. Serve at your church relentlessly. Don't listen to this culture say that you are devalued because you are single. Get to work – this time has endless possibilities.

Third, don't settle. If you want to avoid getting stuck with a dud instead of a stud (sorry, I couldn't resist), then do this activity for me. Write down on a piece of paper or even in this book a specific list. Ask this question: if my Heavenly Father were selecting a spouse for me, what traits would he require him to have? Start listing them out. You can come up with a pretty intense list, and once you do, resolve not to waver from it. He has your best interest in mind; you need to trust him.

Fourth, don't over-spiritualize the process (but also don't leave God out of the equation either). Too many people are awaiting a divine revelation to explode through the clouds. Oftentimes, God simply wants you to find someone who obeys his Word, and then he allows you to use godly wisdom to discern if this is the right person or not.

Finally, remember the "Love Triangle." God sits at the top of the triangle. A fellow on the left side, a lady on the right side, and we have a complete triangle. If the fellow decides to grow close to the lady, he neglects his relationship with God, but if he chooses to grow close to God, and she chooses the same thing, they grow closer together as well. If you think that concept is too simplistic or too spiritual of an answer, let me ask you something: Have you ever seen a person's life spiritually deteriorate because he or she focused more on a relationship with a boyfriend or a girlfriend than he or she did on God? We all have. It happens all the time. If mission does not define the relationship, then the relationship will determine the mission.

Choose wisely.

Group Questions

Chapter 4: the Date

*If mission does not define the relationship,
then the relationship will define the mission.*

1. Think about the worst couple dating you know. What makes their relationship so unhealthy?

2. What mission do you believe God has you on earth to do?

3. What type of person could best help you fulfill that mission?

4. Read 1 Corinthians 7:32-35. If God's desire is that you possess undistracted devotion to the Lord, do you think you could better do that single or married? Why?

5. Make a list of the type of godly spouse that your Heavenly Father would desire you to have. Once you have this list, do not settle.

Pray that you not settle for anything less than God's best. And pray that you become the godly person now that your spouse will need one day.

the **Purity**

Any step away from God will always be too far.

When I was seven years old, the only thing that I wanted for Christmas was cowboy boots. I don't know if it was because Billy Ray Cyrus' mullet was literally sweeping across the nation or because a family friend was letting me ride his horses, but I desperately needed cowboy boots to survive in my seven-year old world. I found the perfect pair too – black leather with red curly stripes up the side. I asked Santa Claus for them at the mall, but a dilemma arose.

At the second grade lunch table, conversation had been arising amongst us young lads. The serious crisis that had gripped our conversation over Salisbury steak, tater tots, and juice bars had been none other than the elusive Santa Claus. Some of my friends had become increasingly skeptical, and so our council ensued.

Taylor stated that there was no Santa Claus. He had stumbled upon a Santa plush wardrobe in his dad's closet just last Christmas. When he asked his older brother, he told him that it was stupid to believe in Santa Claus. So we had convicting evidence and an older, more experienced witness. On the defense side, Eric woke up last Christmas and snuck in his living room to find Santa putting out toys, only then to see his dad walk in the room alongside Santa. So the father conspiracy was refuted, but still doubts lingered and basically none of us could sleep at night anymore.

On a fateful December Saturday, I was doing chores at the house with my sister. I was dusting around the mantle when all of a sudden I caught a glimpse of some unusual colors behind the fireplace cover. I leaned it back and saw a huge stack of toys. I grabbed my older sister and showed her. We began to grow in excitement until we heard my mom walking down the hall to which we flung back the cover and tried to act as if we were still cleaning. With a suspicious glare, Mom then instructed us to leave the room.

Upon gaining access for reentry, she reminded us to continue our chores as she left that day and not to touch anything that wasn't ours. That was easy enough. She left; we watched her car pull down the driveway as we crawled to the living room window, and then we made a dash for the loot. For after all, we weren't going to touch anything that wasn't ours or at least that wouldn't be ours.

A karaoke machine was there. Teenage Mutant Nina Turtles were coming out of the woodwork, and there at the bottom of that luscious stack were the black cowboy boots with red curly stripes up the side. As I began to jump up and down due to the overwhelming excitement, I also caught a glimpse of something else in that pile. On top of that pile of sweet goodness was a note from my mother that read: "If you mess with my stuff, you will never ever see it again."

Upon reading this note, my sister and I went into a state of panic that rivaled any the world had ever seen. We begin to look for video cameras, clean for fingerprints, investigate for bomb triggers we might have set off, and made sure that everything was exactly as we had found it. We closed the cover and dared never to mention this again.

My mom came home, and we remained cool upon her arrival. Nothing was ever said about the note. A couple of weeks later, it was Christmas morning. After waking up very early, I ran down the hall on Christmas morning to see the cowboy boots that I always wanted, and something strange happened – I had to make myself appear happy and surprised. I knew Santa hadn't given them, and I also knew the only magic in our chimney was that note that sent my sister and me running for our lives. What should have been an incredible moment was good, but it wasn't stellar. I still put the boots on and wore them till I couldn't wear them anymore, but some of the excitement was lost somewhere in beholding something destined to be mine just a little too early.

Our sexuality is a lot like those cowboy boots. God designed it so that he would give us this incredible gift of sex with one partner for an entire life, but every peek and every encounter with that gift before the time he has designated to give that gift takes away some of the nostalgia and fulfillment purposed to accompany sex. It diminishes with every date that gets a little too physical. The gift loses some of its luster every time an inappropriate website is visited. It loses some of its appeal every sexual compromise that we commit.

Now don't be confused, I still loved wearing my cowboy boots even though I was premature about seeing them, but they could not be enjoyed in the perfect way that the giver intended. For those of you who have messed up sexually, that fact does not mean that you will not enjoy the gift of sex once or if you get married. All I am saying is that every premature messing around with that gift before the Giver intended to give it diminishes the power of that gift. The fifth way to give Jesus weight in your life is to obey his commands concerning personal purity.

"How Far is Too Far?"

If you didn't struggle sexually in your youthful years, count yourself part of the minority. Just to state the obvious: the struggle for purity in college grows in intensity. The freedom of what you watch, whom you see, where you sleep, how you dress, and what you do increases dramatically. And while many of you were excited about leaving the nest and not having to deal with overbearing parents, a stark reality is that safe havens from temptation are few and far between during your college years.

"So how far is too far?". The problem with that question is that it is a self-referentially absurd question. If you want to know the answer to this question, you are asking a bad question. In a sense, if premarital sex or adultery is the ultimate sexual sin, you want to know how close you can get to that and still be OK. Let's be honest: you are asking how far you can pleasurably enjoy the things that caused Jesus to be brutally killed.

The goal is not to see how close you can get to sin. The goal is to be holy because God is holy (1 Pet. 1:16). We don't want to get near sin;

we should yearn to flee from it. The problem is that many people have never decided concerning the area of purity what is actually classified as sin. You don't know how far is too far. If you don't determine how far is too far, you will cross the line every time. All logic is thrown out the window when we are experiencing temptation. Temptation leads to lust; lust leads to sin; and sin leads to death (James 1:14-15). You must determine what is off limits and what is free game when it comes to your sexual activity in college, and if you don't have an authority to help determine the line, you will never know when to stop.

That's why I propose that the road to holiness in the area of sexual purity can be found in "The Duct-Tape Standard of Holiness." Imagine a line of duct tape (since every college student knows that duct tape fixes everything) in your college dorm room scaling one side all the way to the other side (a whopping three inches). On the far right side, that part of the tape represents totally pure sexuality. This side is so pure that nuns would call you asking you how you stay so innocent. On the far left side, that part represents a rebellion against God's instructions for sex so great that Jerry Springer himself wouldn't even have you on his show because you make *him* feel uncomfortable.

Let's imagine that you are standing on the pure side. How far is too far going down the line? You must be aware that the nature of our sexual desire is a lot like the law of diminishing returns. Once you held hands with someone for the first time, you were enamored with butterflies swarming in your stomach. Your first kiss sent your knees knocking. The problem is we always leave wanting something more. We are designed that way.

If you are honest, some of you reading are already flooded with thoughts, actions, habits, and mistakes that you have committed. You might say that you are somewhere in the middle of this duct tape measurement of purity. Maybe you can't erase the pornographic images from your mind that you stumbled upon or sought after on the Internet. Maybe you left your last date ridden with guilt entertaining the idea that you went too far physically in the car, but you're too scared to tell your date of your dilemma due to the possible repercussions. Or possibly you bought into the lie that masturbation is acceptable because if you didn't do that, you would commit a "worse" sexual sin. You can't miss your favorite television show but wouldn't dare think of watching it with your pastor in the room. Maybe you realized that modest dressing doesn't get you attention, but as soon as you revealed some of yourself, those crushes of yours finally began to take notice.

Or perhaps you've thought about cleaning out your movie library but just can't get rid of some of them with a favorite scene. You might have entertained lustful thoughts about someone of the same sex. Gradually you lowered your standards in order to keep your boyfriend or girlfriend because you don't want to be lonely. Maybe you have purchased a magazine you've got hidden, frequented a strip club, bought an internet cleaning program to destroy evidence, deliberated that oral sex wasn't that bad, or maybe you are engaging in sex with the person you're "going" to marry, and so it would be foolish for you to stop.

So how far is too far? Paul gives us a hint. In Ephesians 5:3, Paul states that among Christians there should "not be even a hint of sexual immorality, or of any kind of impurity." Before we study the implications of that standard, we must understand God's heart on this issue first.

God is More Pro-Sex Than Anybody

I thought that might get your attention, but that statement is foundationally true. God is more pro-sex than anybody. Who is the Creator of sex? God. So who should answer our questions concerning sex? God. So who did God create sex for? Here is an interesting point – sex is designed to be enjoyed the fullest within the context of Christian marriage, and yet Christians are often the least likely to discuss sex.

If you grew up in church or had Christian family members, you possibly heard theology taught like this: "Sex is evil. Sex is bad. Save it for the person that you love." Isn't that romantic?

Maybe we've encountered a polemical dilemma. Sex is not evil; it is beautiful. It is to be extremely enjoyed, and God is the one giving that gift to his children with a smile on his face. With that gift, he gives instructions not to limit or to take away enjoyment, but his instructions concerning sex are prefaced by his heart in saying: "In order to enjoy this to the max, the way that I designed it for you to enjoy in the fullest sense, I've given you some guidelines."

You must understand that your sexual desire is not sinful. Your untimely and improper way of handling your sexual desire is sinful. Sexual cravings are a gift from God, but to truly enjoy those cravings in the proper way, God had to set up some parameters. You may not think that these desires are a gift currently in your single state, for they often seem like a curse due to your inability to properly satisfy those urges.

You must begin to change your philosophy concerning your sexual desires. Sex, the way God intended, brings glory to God. Your sexual relationship with your spouse one day is nothing less than worship to God (some of you are already shouting, "hallelujah"), but like all other things that are beautiful gifts from God, sin cheapens the gift when we choose to disobey God's instructions.

Going to the Chapel

Before you can enjoy sex in the confines of a great marriage relationship, you are always slowly moving your way towards the chapel. You are nearing marriage. For those of you dating someone, the difficulty surrounding purity in a long-term dating relationship becomes evermore intense. The very nature of a relationship is to grow more intimately. A friendship becomes stagnate when you aren't going deeper emotionally or socially. A dating relationship is just the same except that it also has this sphere of sexuality attached to it. After you have kissed your date for a certain interval of time ranging from one-second to four and a half hours, you are unwilling to resort to anything less sensual that what you have previously experienced. You always want something more. So many Christian couples that date for a long time find the only unexplored area in their relationship is sexual. In the natural progression of growing closer, they begin to lose their standard of how far is too far.

Remember the standard? There should not even be a hint of sexual immorality in your life. The standard is not cultural goodness but godly holiness. The goal is not to be better than other people on campus. The goal is to be holy. Any step away from God will always be too far.

As you grow closer, it is hard to remain content in your relationship before you get married. For the ladies, the most important conversation that will take place in a relationship besides the engagement proposal, is the D.T.R. talk. The D.T.R. is the "Define The Relationship" talk which is often dreaded by guys. Girls want to know where the relationship is heading. What is the guy's future plans and goals? What does he call her when he's around his friends? Guys think this conversation is not necessary. Girls disagree with you and disagree strongly. This conversation is sorely needed because ladies often need that security to know where they stand in their relationships.

The most important conversation for a guy to initiate is concerning how far is too far in a couple's physical relationship. This conversation is the E.T.B. or the "Establish The Boundaries" talk. When I normally encourage a guy to do this with his girlfriend, he comes close to passing out. It is an awkward conversation, but it is necessary, and the talk must be specific.

You always want something more...In the natural progression of growing closer, they begin to lose their standard of how far is too far.

Let me explain why this talk is so important. I will often talk with college students who are shameful of their dating relationship progressing too much sexually. They never distinguished how far too far was in their dating relationship; therefore, they crossed it every night they were together. The Spirit of God convicts true believer, and they both feel shameful after the incident, but since they never talk about it, they keep messing up, and they keep progressively getting too far down the Duct Tape Standard of Holiness.

A buddy of mine in college got convicted concerning his physical relationship getting out of hand with his girlfriend. He finally initiated the E.T.B. conversation, and he was heartbroken to hear his girlfriend's response. She was a fairly new Christian, and her boyfriend had been a Christian for many years. When he told her his conviction, she responded, "I've thought what we were doing was wrong for a long time, but since I knew that you were closer to God than me, I figured I was just wrong because surely you would have stopped it if we were actually sinning."

Ashamed and regretful, he continued the E.T.B. talk, and they got practical about establishing boundaries within their relationship. If you are in a relationship, you need to initiate the E.T.B. talk. The awkwardness is not nearly as uncomfortable as the regret associated with continually indulging in sin. Get specific about what is off limits. You probably need to set up parameters concerning how much kissing and cuddling you can do with each other. Many couples struggle more late at night when their defense is down, so maybe you need to decide what times your date will always end by.

Many of you need to consider that you are also to flee from the very appearance of evil (1 Th. 5:22). Not only are you not to sin, but you shouldn't appear to be sinning. If your girlfriend sleeps on your couch when she comes to visit you, what is causing your neighbors to think you aren't sleeping with her? Why would they think otherwise? If you watch movies in your apartment together late at night with the lights off, what is keeping people who are looking for an excuse not to follow Christ to find a great excuse in your appearance of evil. I know its hard, and you want to hang out with one another. People are going to think what they want to, but you don't have to help them think even worse things. You have to decide which is more important to you: a passing moment of comfort or the expansion of the Kingdom of God on your campus?

The Danger of Lust

Unfortunately, sins dealing with purity do not only happen within the confines of a dating relationship. Many sexual sins never take fruition outside of someone's mind. Jesus raised the bar in a sermon once. He realized the people acknowledged that adultery was a sin, but he stated, "I say to you that everyone who looks at a woman with lustful intent has already committed adultery with her in his heart" (Matt. 5:27-28). It's not only what we do sexually that affects us (1 Cor. 6:18), but what we think about also has devastating effects on our purity (2 Cor. 10:5).

The lust of the eyes (1 John 2:16) cripples most guys. Men are more visually stimulated, and our culture is not exactly excelling in the modesty category. Lust is not solely specific to guys though. Lust is not sexist and can attack anyone in different forms. According to Jesus' statements, sins rebelling from a pure lifestyle can happen physically with someone else or all by yourself.

The internet is full of sexually provocative sites and ads that constantly drive men and women away from purity. Even for people not searching for explicit material can find it displayed through social networking sites. Love scenes on television and in the movies get more and more risqué by the year giving minds unrealistic expectations producing unholy consequences. Even though the temptation seems to get greater by the day, we must remember that any sexual fulfillment that does not fall into line with God's boundaries is nothing less than sin. Even if the sin only happens in our mind or with no one else around, God is aware and still treats it as sin.

If you truly want to succeed in the purity department, you are going to have to decide to fight lust at all costs. While I was in college, I started fighting back. First, I went to God with repentance whenever I sinned. I never wanted to get calloused about disobeying God (Eph. 4:19). Second, I got an accountability partner. I knew on my best days I was still a sinner and had the possibility of doing something stupid and ruining my witness, and so I needed a person to ask me the tough questions. I even made the questions out for him. Every week, my buddy and I would meet for lunch, and he asked me the same questions concerning my devotional life, my dating relationship, my media intake, and my thought life. It was tough to look at him in the eyes and give him honest answers sometimes, but there is a worse scenario: having to face everyone in my life with answers if I royally messed up. I figured I would rather lose my reputation with that one guy than everyone who knew me.

Third, I memorized Scripture in any needed areas as weapons in the fight (Eph. 6:17). In those moments of temptation, I knew God could rescue me (1 Cor. 10:13), and I meditated on verses on purity so that if I did sin, it was going to be a fight (Ps. 119:9). Fourth, I never closed my doors at college. This one may seem funny to you, but it was a lifesaver. Since sexual media was just a click away on my computer, I always had my doors open. I never locked my doors, and I told people that they always had open access to my room. Finally, I got an Internet software called X3 Watch that sent emails to my accountability partners if I ever viewed a questionable site. I choose my pastor and one my best friends so that I would be utterly humiliated if I ever looked at something unholy. If you are in a battle, you must decide to fight.

Modest is Hottest

Concerning the sins of the mind and the heart, one issue that needs to be addressed is that of decent clothing. One day my roommate, affectionately called Freaky P., came in our dorm room outraged. Springtime was budding, which meant it was that special time of year when girls are able to stop wearing clothes that cover again. As a result, Christian guys fighting for purity love the wintertime.

He was trying to make his way from class to our dorm room at our Christian college in safety, but he was attacked. Godly girls spiritually attacked him by the un-sanctified lack of clothing that they were wearing. He was so enraged that he decided to write an editorial to our college's newspaper, the *Skyliner*. They published the letter which was a scriptural explanation of purity and a plea for girls to consider their Christian brothers in how they dressed.

On the day that the paper came out, many people found Freaky P. and thanked him for his honesty and his boldness. Many girls approached him and acknowledged how he had challenged them, except for one. We'll call her the Devil. As she approached her seat in class in front of my roommate, she commented that she had read his article today. She then proceeded to lean over his desk, pull up her shirt to her neck, and ask, "what's the matter Phillip, does this make you stumble?"

Now if I had the privilege to obtain the power of God for one day and it just happened to be that day, she would be dead. OK, I probably wouldn't have killed her. Probably. I would have provided her a sex change for about twenty-four hours, and I would get her to live in a body that is so visually stimulated surrounded by beautiful women who seem bent to reveal themselves more and more, and then I would ask her to reconsider her callous, destructive comments and behavior.

Sin is not cute. Sin kills, and if anyone is that flippant about sin, you need to sincerely examine yourself to see whether or not you are in the faith.

I used to tell my wife, Amanda, that if girls only knew what went on in guys' lustful minds, they would wear parkas in the summer. I would try to explain to her how guys are so visually stimulated, and if girls only knew that, they would refrain from wearing certain clothing or the lack thereof. She corrected me by saying that most girls do know what is going on in guys' heads, and that's why they wear what they wear.

Amanda told me that girls realize that guys start paying them more attention the more scandalously they dress, and so that provides them the needed motivation. Since one of a woman's greatest needs is to experience the security associated with a relationship, oftentimes, ladies will do whatever it takes to get that relationship. If it means showing more than they should show in order to get attention, that is a small price to pay for a woman who is desiring a long-term relationship.

Since she refuted the parka argument, I decided to come up with a new line of reasoning. This argument is what I like to call "The Wardrobe Malfunction Case Study." Our first example we will call Christian Guy. Christian Guy's daily goal is to keep his eyes on Christ. He is growing spiritually, and he desperately wants to please Jesus in all that he does and concerning what he thinks about.

Our second example we will call Shady Cat. Shady Cat has a popped collar on his polo shirt. His walk and overuse of body spray gives him away. You can spot this guy out in a crowd because he is jumping up and down to be the center of it. Shady Cat's daily goal is to be an absolute moron. All he knows is shade; therefore, he is Shady Cat.

If you were to bring in Wardrobe Malfunction Girl, two things would happen: 1) Christian Guy would keep his eyes on Christ; he has a desire to look, but he tries to fight the temptation, and 2) Shady Cat would indulge, for he is and shall always be a Shady Cat. Let's say that Wardrobe Malfunction Girl and Shady Cat get married. They both get old and gain a few extra pounds when one day Wardrobe Malfunction Girl #2 enters the scene that looks a lot better than his aged wife. What would he do? Shady Cats will always leave because if it took sexual temptation to get him attracted to you, that very thing will be the catalyst that takes him away.

Be careful how you advertise, ladies. Your dress will get you a man, but I don't know if it's the kind of man you are going to want for the long haul. If you truly want a godly man, understand that one who is trying to live a pure life will not desire a lady who is showing the world half of what should be revealed on her wedding night.

Homosexuality

I do not have enough space in this book to delve in a debate concerning why or why not homosexuality is a sin. If you are developing your worldview from the Bible, then you must accept homosexual relationships as sinful. I hate that many Christians have isolated homosexuality as the worst sin of all; James said that if we messed up in one area, we are guilty of all sins (James 2:10). While there are plenty of sins of a heterosexual nature, homosexual relationships are always biblically out of bounds.

I have talked with many practicing homosexuals who say they were born that way. I will agree with that statement to a point in the sense that we were born to sin. If I was born greedy, that desire could lead me to steal. If I was born with a temper, those feelings could lead me to kill someone. If I was born with an unholy tendency to lust, those feelings could lead me to rape. A person can be born with homosexual tendencies, but that does not mean those feelings are from God any more than anger comes from God. We cannot follow our feelings to their natural conclusions. It will and always does lead to sin. Homosexual relationships are sinful since they are not in accordance with God's plan.

"If You Love Me, You Will..."

In the area of purity, I have often hear of a couple who say that they messed up physically. Their standard was not holiness, and they went too far, and a lot of those encounters are based upon a boyfriend or girlfriend saying, "If you love me, you will..." Normally, that statement follows having sex or performing some other sexual act. It's interesting that the beginning of that phrase is similar to a statement of Jesus. That's why I give young ladies a response if a guy ever states, "If you love me, you'll have sex with me."

Ladies, you reply, "Jesus said, 'If you love me, you will obey what I command'" (John 14:15). If you really love someone, you will obey Christ's commands because he's written the book on sex and knows how it is supposed to be used. Anyone who gives you an ultimatum likes that deserves a John 14:15 roundhouse kick to the head.

You know what I think would help a lot of Christians out in their quest for purity? If you would stop viewing those around you as sexual objects, you could begin to view them as spiritual beings instead. Too often college Bible studies are filled with guys and girls that are lurking through a room eyeing out potential prospects versus seeing those around them as their brothers and sisters in Christ. If you follow Christ, and keep holiness as your standard, one day you are going to be able to open up the gift the way the Giver intended, and you will be glad you waited because the best things in life truly do come to those who wait.

Any step away from God will always be too far.

Group Questions

Chapter 5: **the Purity**

Any step away from God will always be too far.

1. How would the students on your campus determine how far is too far?

2. What are some ways that you can continue to grow closer in a relationship without compromising sexually?

3. If you are in a relationship now or hope to be in one (please, God, some day soon), what boundaries should you set up?

4. Read Matthew 5:27-30. How does Jesus' stance on purity differ from our culture's or even our churches'?

5. How can you practically combat sin in your quest for purity? How can you protect yourself?

    Pray that you wait to be given God's gift in his own timing. Pray that you will not cheapen his gift by going about it your own way.

the **Party Scene**

Love limits freedom.

When I was in elementary school, my family moved from our small apartment into a house with a great big backyard. With this amount of space, there was only one thing missing at our new residence. We needed a dog.

My sister and I begged and pleaded, and we promised our mom that we could handle the responsibility associated with raising dogs even though we were unsure of what that actually entailed. We visited a kennel where the owner had dogs galore jam packed in tiny cages. My sister, four years my senior, went and picked out a shaggy-haired mutt named Butch. When they let the puppies loose for me to pick one, I became scared of all the rambunctious dogs except for the runt of the litter, Pepper. That's right, I admitted it. I used to be scared of dogs, but I gradually adjusted to the mutt and to the runt. So off we drove them to their new home and rescued them from those awful living conditions and set them down in a backyard the size of a football field plentifully stocked with all the food, water, and space they could ever possibly desire.

They loved it. We loved them. Everything was great in our flea-infested world – until the neighborhood stray dogs came around.

They ran up to the fence, and a lot of barking transpired. Upon their arrival, I noticed something in Butch's eyes. A sparkle began to emerge under his unkempt hair that was troubling. Here, amidst doggy paradise, Butch began to permit a question to linger in his heart: "Is there more to life that I'm missing out here in this confining backyard?"

He envied the freedom of the stray dogs. He coveted their carefree attitude, and all of a sudden the protection that he benefited from became the barrier that confined him. One fateful night, he made a run for it. He dug a hole underneath the fence and attempted to quench his rebellious thirst. We didn't see him for two days.

Then one afternoon, we received a call. Butch had been spotted rummaging through neighbors' yards and chasing after feline nuisances. We went to go track him down, and we brought him back to the security of the backyard. Even though we were tempted, we never withheld his food or his water. We still showered him with affection. Due to his charismatic nature and shaggy hair, we just couldn't stay mad at him for too long.

Then he left again, and he left again. Actually, he had a steady routine of digging a new hole every time that I patched up one of his old escape routes. Something assured him that he would always have a home here regardless of how many times he would run away. He knew that we would always provide for him, and somehow, that was just too safe and predictable for him, and so he needed more. Thus was the story of Butch the Mutt all of his days – secure in his home, yet rebellious in his living.

Longing for Freedom

I have to admit that there is a little bit of Butch in me. Since I became a Christian, adopted from my wretched state, I have had the absolute best conditions provided. I have received divine protection from the outside world, and I have never gone without my needs being adequately met. I have experienced all the love, affection, and security I could ever imagine, and yet somehow, that provision sinisterly becomes boring to me; I long for something more.

I'm not talking about jumping off the deep end spiritually. I don't want to renounce my commitment to Christ. I don't want to fall into a state of moral failure; I just sometimes get tired of these fences. I look through the fence of God's commands to see the carefree hearts of those straying on the outside, and I envy their blithe state. Amidst unbelievable scenery, gifts, and the love of my Master, I just want to be able to indulge a moment where I just let go. I want freedom.

You do too. Honestly, there is that longing in all of us that started when we were a child. When we couldn't do what we wanted to, we would turn and ask our parents, "Why?" No matter how many times we heard the excuse, "Because I said so," that explanation was unable to cut it. We are born knowing what we think is the best for us, and we dare anyone to challenge that ideal.

One of the most debated issues in Christianity concerning freedom is that of social drinking. Denominations differ. Backgrounds divide. Experiences direct. When most pastors communicate to students concerning the sins to abstain from in America, the list normally starts with premarital sex, drinking, and smoking. These are areas which the Bible actually does address, but few ministers ever mention the sins of hating one's brother, developing an envious heart, supplanting God for another, etc. Why has the American church focused so much on the previous? It is that these actions are observable, concrete practices while so many other areas are matters of the heart. I can physically see if someone is drinking alcohol or not. I cannot perceive whether or not someone has bitterness in the heart towards another.

Many people who want to live for Christ see the party scene on the outside, and they envy it. They envy the carefree nature, and you begin to wonder: is drinking really evil, or am I just listening to my fuddy-duddy preacher and parents way too much? It's the seduction of the unknown.

Most students, upon their first taste of alcohol, do not rave about the mesmerizing flavor, but they do come back for some reason. Some come back because people they admired accepted them for the first time. Some try it again because it made them forget about all the drama in their lives. Some continue to indulge because the Christian cliques on campus ostracized them for the first time they went to a party, so now they have nowhere else to turn.

So now you allow the question to run rampant in your mind: "Is there more to life that I'm missing by associating with Christianity?" So is it wrong to drink? Can a Christian go to a party? Can he socially drink?

As our culture progresses, the line keeps getting blurrier. Not only do different churches and Christians disagree on this issue, but also it appears as if the Bible supports both sides or is at least ambiguous about the topic. So to address this issue, I encourage you to lay aside your tradition, denomination, preconceived notions, parental instruction, parental example, and join me in looking at what God's Word really says about the issue of alcohol.

"Wine for the Stomach?"

Whenever this discussion is brought up, someone normally joins in and says that Paul told Timothy it was OK to drink. For all the people who have alluded to that verse without knowing its actual location, here goes: 1 Timothy 5:23 states: "No longer drink water exclusively, but use a little wine for the sake of your stomach and your frequent ailments." It appears here that Paul is advocating the consumption of alcohol. Now before any of you bingers out there decide to memorize that as your life verse, let's see what's really going on in this passage. What's important to note is that earlier in this letter Paul instructed his son in the faith, Timothy, to have leaders in the church that were above reproach in their moral integrity. You know what one of the qualifications for the elders and the deacons to serve was? They could not be drunkards (1 Tim. 3:3, 8). So from this passage, we at least see Paul telling Timothy to drink wine for his health, but he was not to put anyone in spiritual leadership who constantly drank a substantial amount of alcohol.

I've heard a lot of people find allowance for alcohol in the fact that Jesus turned water into wine. Opponents to social drinking will reply, "He might have turned it into wine, but you never see him drinking it." If you are unfamiliar with the story, let me explain it. In John 2, Jesus' first recorded miracle is at a wedding. The hosts of the wedding run out of the wine, and Jesus' mama comes up and tells him about the situation wanting him to do something. Jesus turns the water into wine, and apparently, Jesus knows how to brew well because the party is raving about this batch being the best they have consumed all day.

Some people have claimed that the wine that Jesus transformed was something more like grape juice and that wine in that day was really not alcohol. That assumption is simply incorrect. Jesus did not turn water into Welch's grape juice, but he didn't turn it into a Colt 45 either. If you're like me, you look at these two passages, and you still walk away without a conclusive argument about whether or not you can go to a keg party on Saturday night and go to the late service at church on Sunday morning without feeling guilty.

The Bible on Drunkenness

What does the Bible say concerning alcohol concretely? Here's what we know without a doubt: first, drunkenness is frowned upon. While biblical alcohol is not completely parallel to the stuff served at your campus' parties, wine was a part of life for many in biblical times. Without a doubt, the consumption of too much alcohol always had a negative effect within the pages of the Bible. What is too much alcohol? Is there a blood count level that the Bible prescribes to steer clear? Unfortunately, there is not, but there is example upon example to allow us to form a pretty safe rule: if your wine consumption could cause you to do something you regret later, that is an unwise amount.

Let's take the first account in the Bible concerning alcohol. Noah has been chosen to lead the only family that God wasn't going to obliterate on the earth, and so he takes his family and all the animals (they came in by twosies, twosies) onto the ark before the flood comes. When the waters subside, Noah, his family, and all the animals debark from the boat. God tells them to live it up on the earth and repopulate it. He tells them that every time they see a rainbow in the sky, they should remember his promise that he won't destroy the earth again (at least by a flood). They have a worship service, and then Noah gets plastered.

Granted, if I had been stuck on a boat with the lovely aroma of all his beastly shipmates for as long as he did, I might have hit the bottle too. Noah decides to begin the first moonshine company recorded in the Bible. He makes a vineyard, he indulges himself with the fruit of his labor, he gets hammered, and then he gets naked. That description sounds a lot like some of the college parties going on in the States actually. Often college parties will either climax with some guy hurting himself, the party getting busted, or somebody starts getting in the nude.

In Noah's case, the response sounds sort of familiar too. One of his sons, unfortunately named Ham, incites his other brothers in an attempt to humiliate his father. He thinks the whole incident is hilarious, but his brothers aren't as amused. Ham's two brothers actually try to cover up their father's shame. Covering up his shame biblically represents their attempt at putting clothes back on their dad without seeing or touching anything that could scar them for the rest of their lives. Ham actually is punished for making light of his father's situation, while the other two brothers are blessed (Gen. 9:20-27).

Noah's incident is pretty bad, but in the Bible, alcohol is also attributed to many other sinful practices. God once said that wine was robbing his people of their senses because they were making horrible decisions partially due to their alcohol consumption (Hos. 4:11). In the Book of Proverbs, a father tells a son not to associate with those people who drink too much since their lives will end in poverty (Prov. 23:19-21). The author even states that if someone drinks too much, he is a person who is constantly complaining and always feeling sorry for himself (Prov. 23:29). He even warns that alcohol will be tempting, but you will pay severely in the morning with a hangover (Prov. 23:31-32). Who knew the Bible talked about hangovers? The Bible *is* relevant to my campus!

When God's people were in serious trouble, God traced the problem back to their leaders consuming too much alcohol that rendered them helpless to make correct spiritual decisions (Isa. 28:7). In the Bible, kings who forgot to take care of the people's needs were those kings who drank too much (Prov. 31:5). The Bible is full of bad choices stemming from liquor.

As seen in the Bible, normally when alcohol is present, crazy things happen. Oftentimes, they are regretful occurrences. College parties are often known for someone doing something ridiculous, others making fun of him, and then that person wakes up the next morning not only with a hangover but also pictures of himself shamefully doing his stunts all over Facebook. Usually, he has no recollection of the event. The

Bible clearly shows that drunkenness is not something in which to aspire, but it also shows that making light of someone's state is also unhealthy.

Second, we know that drunkenness is often listed in a group of sins from which Christians should abstain. Drunkenness is seen as counterproductive to the fruits of the Spirit (Ga. 5:21). At parties, how many people have you seen display self-control, peace, or kindness? Sure you may have seen them display joy, but I don't think drunken hysteria can be equated to biblical joy. Keg parties seriously lack any element of self-control. No one knows where the line is concerning where it is imperative to stop. You don't know when to stop because you are unable to think clearly. In fact, most parties are not only void of self-control, but also full of pressure to resist self-control encouraging one another to drink even more. In the last years, our nation has seen numerous deaths on college campuses because drunk friends encouraged someone not to stop for the sake of a few laughs.

In Eph. 5:18, we are warned not to cheapen our lives by getting drunk. Paul equated it as literally cheapening our lives by drinking ourselves to a state of confusion. He did state that we are to be filled with the Holy Spirit instead. As a child of God, we are to be directed by the Holy Spirit with his governing and directing every action. When alcohol gets out of control, we are no longer directed by the Holy Spirit, but by a cheapened state of ourselves.

Third, we know that Christian leaders' lives are not to be characterized by a large or consistent amount of alcohol. I already mentioned that Paul told Timothy not to put people in church leadership that were hooked on the bottle. He didn't want anyone making spiritual decisions that affected others if they couldn't even make wise decisions regarding themselves on when to stop drinking.

The Culture's View

Even if Christians disagree about alcohol consumption, our culture consistently holds that Christianity and alcohol are in contradiction to one another. For some people outside the faith, they are constantly searching for an excuse of why they don't have to convert to be a Christian. On college campuses, I have been amazed at how many non-Christians criticize Christians for drinking indicating that there is no different between that person and those Christians.

I have also witnessed many Christian organizations be sidelined for years due to the leaders of that organization hitting up the party scene in the middle of the year. If nonbelievers are searching for an excuse so that they don't have to change their lives, this reason is recurring on every campus in America. When leaders of campus organizations are found to be lacking in integrity by preaching one way and living completely differently, it actually makes the task of bringing the gospel to that campus even harder because now people have an extra excuse. Paul knew what he was talking about warning against leaders who were consistently partying. Not only does it affect the way they lead, but it also harms the reputation of the whole organization trying to reach out to a campus who needs Jesus.

The Bible is also consistent in encouraging God's people to always make the wisest choice when confronted with multiple options. Solomon made it clear when he stated that "wine is a mocker, strong drink a brawler, and whoever is intoxicated by it is not wise" (Prov. 20:1). Have you ever seen alcohol cause someone to turn into a mocker or a brawler? It happens all the time. Someone gets a little too much of the goods in their system, and all of a sudden they are saying some horrendous things about people that they would never say if they were sober. They confess things that should not even be revealed to Oprah and Dr. Phil. They declare feelings that they won't even pen in a journal, and while that person does that, the person's best friends just allow it to happen all in good fun.

Beer is definitely a brawler. Fights break out, and alcohol is normally one of the components. When a person's alcohol level is high, he is unable to truly judge how he feels or responsibly react to what is happening around him. Due to these reasons, Solomon just claims that if alcohol causes humiliation and anger, then it is simply unwise for a child of God to be intoxicated by it because it makes normally wise people do stupid things. Of all people, Solomon should know. He persistently indulged in alcohol to cheer himself up (Ecc. 2:3), but he ended up saying that it was a worthless, meaningless pursuit because it could not provide him satisfaction (Ecc. 2:11).

Based on the examples we have seen, if we derive our worldview from the teaching of Scripture, we have to at least say that drunkenness is disobedience to God. Disobedience to God is sin. A true follower of Jesus does not continue on knowingly in sin without any conviction or attempt for improvement (1 John 3:9).

As a side note, this debate shouldn't even be an issue for some of you reading. If you are under the legal age of alcohol consumption, it should definitely not even be in question for under-age drinkers. I am shocked at how many claim that they are free to do it, and they are under the legal age of drinking. Read Romans 13:1 to see how God's Word instructs us to be obedient to the governing authorities that he put over us. If you are of age but you belong to a dry campus or organization, you should also honor that institution's standards and submit to their policies. Part of our witness in this world is to allow our outstanding behavior in society to draw people to God (1 Pt. 2:13-15).

Out of the college students with whom I talk, some students know that drunkenness is bad, and they keep doing it. In fact, some of them are so used to getting that fix from alcohol consumption that they are slowly becoming alcoholics even if they don't realize it, but there remains another group I want to address as well. These are the students that live for Christ. They read their Bible, attend church, and even go on mission trips. They never get "drunk," but they will socially drink.

 The right to drink for some comes from an argument based upon "Christian liberty." The verse that they are casually quoting comes from 1 Cor. 6:12 where Paul says: "All things are lawful for me." But most people don't finish his thought where he states that not all things are beneficial. He also states that he will not be mastered by anything. In Christ, we may have the "rights" to do certain things, but does it make it beneficial? And how do you know if you will be mastered by it or not? How do you know if you could be one of the many that gets addicted?

In college, I struggled a lot with this issue; I had a lot of guys that I looked up to who lived for God but would drink a beer or two at a friend's house while hanging out. They never saw it as anything harmful to the Body of Christ, but they just all got together and had a couple of cold ones. I believed that they really were not hurting anyone and I can't make a strong case from the Bible that what they were doing was sinful, so why didn't I just indulge as well?

For me, I resolved the issue in my mind by looking to a situation that Paul had to address a few chapters over from the previous verse. In 1 Corinthians 8, Paul was confronting the Corinthian church about a problem in their congregation. Some people were upset that people were eating meat that had been sacrificed and used in the worship of idols. Translation: this food had been used in worship to foreign gods, and then Christians were eating it. Paul said in 1 Cor. 8:4, "Therefore concerning the eating of things sacrificed to idols, we know that there is no such thing as an idol in the world, and that there is no God but one." So even if he did eat of that food, he knew that in his Christian liberty, he was in essence not doing anything wrong at all.

He then states in v. 9-13: "But take care that this liberty of yours does not somehow become a stumbling block to the weak. For if someone sees you, who has knowledge, dining in an idol's temple, will not his conscience, if he is weak, be strengthened to eat things sacrificed to idols? For through your knowledge he who is weak is ruined, the brother for whose sake Christ died. And so, by sinning against the brethren and wounding their conscience when it is weak, you sin against Christ. Therefore, if food causes my brother to stumble, I will never eat meat again, so that I will not cause my brother to stumble."

> Love limits freedom. He would rather do the loving thing for the sake of others than he would do the "free" thing for the sake of himself.

What is he saying? Paul is stating that he could in fact get away with eating that meat, but for the sake of those younger, more immature believers, he would not do it - even though he could. If he did partake, that action would actually turn into sinning against Christ (1 Cor. 8:12) because it is making his children stumble. So Paul's resolution: I would never do anything that would cause my brother to stumble. Love limits freedom. He would rather do the loving thing for the sake of others than he would do the "free" thing for the sake of himself.

I see that personally, as a direct correlation concerning social drinking. Is it a sin? If you are not getting drunk, it's probably not. The Bible does state that it is unwise (Prov. 20:1), but I can hear people saying now, "Being unwise isn't necessarily sinning." You're right, unless you see how wisdom is portrayed in the beginning of Proverbs - "The fear of the Lord is the beginning of knowledge." (Prov. 1:7). Basically, if you fear the Lord, that's knowledge, and knowledge comes down to being involved in the things that glorify God and not being involved in the activities that could cause another to stumble. "All things are lawful, but not all things are profitable. All things are lawful, but not all things edify." (1 Cor. 10:23). Edifying, building one another up in the Body, is one of the major reasons why we are still on this earth (Eph. 4:12)!

In fact, Jesus actually said that if we caused someone to sin, it would be better for a stone to be wrapped around our neck and sink to the bottom of the sea. While that seems a little extreme, I understand what he means. Let's just say that I decide in my Christian liberty that it is acceptable to drink a glass of wine with my meal at a restaurant. I never drink enough to enable me to swing from the chandeliers or anything, but I just simply drink a few. While I'm at the restaurant, a couple of Christian college students that attend our church's Bible study approach the table to talk. They are spiritual babies. They haven't been walking with Christ for long. But on that night, they see the person who tells them to make everything in their lives about Jesus enjoying life by knocking back a few. They now feel as if it is acceptable for them as well.

That is the cost of spiritual leadership, and even if you aren't in a leadership position, there is somebody looking up to you, and you influence his or her decisions. Let's imagine that those college students leave the restaurant, and since I approved by example the consumption of alcohol, they partake of it as well, but one of them isn't like me. He can't merely drink one or two. He drinks a whole lot more. In fact, he gets addicted to it. He drops out of college because of excessive absences on

Fridays because he is always hung over. He can't get the job he wants. He gets in a relationship, but his girlfriend is always scared of what kind of mood his drinking is going to put him in. If you think I am exaggerating, I'm not. Our church deals with people who started socially drinking, but that soon became insufficient. They needed more. They found more by becoming an alcoholic. Alcohol leads people to addiction, abuse, depression, dependence, murder, and suicide just to name a few.

Where would I trace the beginning of this problem? It all started with my Christian liberty. It all started that I was acting on what I wanted. In the community of faith, I am always to be more concerned with the needs of others than I am my own (Phil. 2:3-4). Love limits freedom. If I love those brothers and sisters of mine, I will forsake some selfish desire for the sake of their spiritual maturity. It's not an issue any longer.

I honestly feel like this group of people who drink under the umbrella of Christian liberty is a lot like my dog Butch. You are doing so many good things, you experience a level of danger when you get to hold a beer bottle in your hand. You are so squeaky clean in so many other areas; you just want to indulge just a little bit. You want to quench your rebellious thirst. You see the fraternities and the sororities that just seem as if they have the most popular students on campus, and they are known for their memorable parties, and you look out of your Christian bubble and you just want to live a little too. You just think that you are free to live it up a little bit, but Peter warned not to use our Christian freedom to cover up our sinful behavior (1 Pet. 2:16).

If you think that the party scene has more to offer than what Christ offers you by following him, you are not fully grasping a relationship with Jesus. Could I drink socially and God not throw lightning bolts at my beer-guzzling body? Probably. Do I want to? Personally, I have chosen to decline. Life is too short to waste time in the gray areas, and certain spiritual lives could be damaged because I choose to embark upon my pursuit of liberty. My liberty isn't worth it to me if it could mean the chance of messing up someone else's spirituality. Love limits freedom, and I love the college students around me too much to mess up their walk for the sake of a passing pleasurable moment that I would probably never remember.

Group Questions

Chapter 6: the Party Scene

Love limits freedom.

1. What arguments for or against alcohol had you heard before reading this chapter?

2. For those who drink on your campus, what are some of the top motivations to indulge in alcohol?

3. What are some of the pros and cons to social drinking?

4. Read 1 Corinthians 8:7-13. How could your decision to drink cause people around you to stumble?

5. If you decided not to drink, what would you actually miss?

Pray for God's direction concerning the party scene. Pray that you will always live with others in mind.

the **Church Hop**

Don't merely attend church, be the church.

I always wondered if the dreaded curse known as "freshman fifteen" was actually a reality. That was until I found myself as a freshmen quickly gaining weight and realizing this concept is not an urban legend but a statement of fact.   At age eighteen, your ability to eat what you want and not show it goes away very quickly. When I was in high school, I ate the same meal in the cafeteria every day. I ate a chicken sandwich, a plate full-o-fries, a sweet tea, and if I was lucky, a juice bar all for the amazing price of $1.10. Life was so good. I ate a healthy snack everyday when I got home of Twinkies, Doritos, and Dr. Pepper, and I never gained a pound.

Then college came. In one measly year, I'm starting to quickly develop what some people are calling "love handles," but they weren't handles, they were more like "love cabinets." I knew I was on my way to the dreaded "fifteen" when an elderly family member of mine saw me over my Christmas Break at college and said as I walked in the door, "You look good, you finally getting fat! Yeah. Fat, fat, fat."

My eating habits hadn't drastically changed.   I didn't eat breakfast in high school; I rarely woke up in time to get any in college. I had never exercised regularly. I didn't watch what I ate because I wasn't fast enough, but all of a sudden, I began to gain weight.

After a while, I did notice a sudden shift. While I never worked out a lot in high school, I was spending a lot more time stagnant in college. I woke up only to sit down in a class. I then came back to the room for two hours and chilled in my room. I went and sat in another class. I then came and played video games for the afternoon. I then studied in a recliner all night. I wasn't moving. The only exercise I was getting was going back for seconds in the cafeteria during Taco Night. I was taking so much in, but I never did anything. I was just a mere statistic on the list of the freshman fifteen plague. I loved eating. I just never did anything. I was enjoying gaining my freshman fifteen and becoming a full-fledged couch potato.

Even worse, I became a spiritual couch potato. It happened on Sunday mornings. It happened at religious organizations on campus. I attended events at which someone "fed" me. I church-hopped on Sunday mornings because I couldn't find a church like my home church. I went to a bunch of religious meetings on campus. I was a spectator. I ate and I ate and I ate, but I never did anything with it. I was religiously fat. I had become a spiritual couch potato who was going back for seconds but never gave any of his food away.

One day, I finally just got sick of it. Something had to change.

Church Options

In college, church hopping is the thing to do. If you are of the minority that continues to go to church once you go out on your own, you visit around different churches during your tenure at college. When you describe your experience, you almost sound as if you are dating around. "Yeah, well the last couple of weeks I've gone and visited this new community church, but if none of my friends are here, I go with my suite mate to that Methodist church near the college." There is little interest and scarce commitment. You really only have a few options concerning church when you are in college:

Neglect. Statistically, this option is the preferred choice of the majority of your campus. Only 20% of your college peers that were active in church during high school remain active in church during college. The rest of your classmates are sleeping in indicating either church has nothing relevant for them or they just personally don't have the commitment level needed.

Hop. Depending upon your relationships, you just go around to different churches your entire college career. If you grew up in a stellar church, this is probably the category in which you will find yourself. Your expectations are so high, which they should be, but you find yourself unable to commit to one because the preacher isn't as approachable as your old one or the music just doesn't do it for you. You hop from church to church.

Spectate. Now this option is primarily for those college students that are attending the hip mega-church. You don't have to dress up, they play secular songs during the prelude, and the speaker constantly refers to cultural fads in order to remain relevant. When you visit these churches, the service is excellent, engaging, and memorable. It's fun and the people you met there are very friendly. You love it. You walk in late, you sit down, enjoy the service, walk out in the parking lot, and you never ever commit to that congregation, and they don't even know if you are there or not from Sunday to Sunday.

Belong. This category is for the person that found an imperfect church, and upon realization that he or she was imperfect as well, jumped in with his or her heart, commitment, time, service, money, and prayers and never looked back. Sure there were things they wished might have been different, but most of those issues were preference related and they had their roots in selfishness. Maybe the other issues that weren't preference related were the very reason they were at that church – to be a positive change-agent. They realized that they were not going to church, but they were the church. They decided to get committed.

Biblical Images

In order to give Jesus weight in this area, you must get committed to a local church. Before I help you find a church, I want to make sure you know what a church is essentially. Upon Peter's correct response to Jesus' inquiry concerning his identity (Matt. 16:16), Jesus told the disciples that he would build his church in such a manner that nothing could overpower it (Matt. 16:18). At this juncture and for a significant time following this incident, Jesus' followers had not yet constructed any buildings in which to gather a community of believers. In fact, many

Christ-followers in the first years of the church's inception were unsure if separation from the Jewish religion was even necessary. In the middle of Christianity's early days, the early church had not yet prescribed essentially what a church was theologically.

Through the teaching of the apostles in the New Testament, believers are to understand the church to be the community of all true believers for all time. The New Testament word for the "church" was *ekklesia*, which simply implied a group gathering or assembly. The word was not originally a religious term as much as it signified a group meeting together for a common purpose. The term is used 111 times in the New Testament. Seventy-three of those times it is specifically referring to the gathering of people, but never does it refer to a building.

As Christianity expanded geographically and exponentially, the writers of the New Testament began to use different inspired illustrations to describe the church. Through these different images, the church was able to better theologically grasp its identity and its purpose during its time upon the earth. If Christ loved the church enough to die for her and intends to grow this church during its tenure on earth, then it is imperative that believers truly understand the biblical descriptions of the church. To better understand the church's function and complexion, one must look at the differing images in an attempt to fully comprehend all of the ensuing implications.

The Family of God. One of the most frequented descriptions of the church in the New Testament is that of the family of God. Due to the commonality and the applicability of this illustration, it is still one of the most frequently used terms by Christians to describe the community of believers. At the head of this family of God, Paul clearly stated to the Ephesian church that God was the church's true, constant father. Since the church's kinship originates from each individual's relationship with his or her father, Paul stated that believers are to treat one another as brothers and sisters. If a person associated himself or herself with God, that person was also assuming a role as a member in God's family.

For the church to understand completely its role as the family of God, the implications drastically change the way the individual members respond to one another's needs during times of crises. As a family,

Christians are expected to behave like members of a loving home by further embracing actions in order to love one another better. A Christian can safely boast of a general concern for the needs at large presently in the world, but Jesus' intention was for Christians to actually apply that love into others' lives by practically meeting their needs. To associate with Christ's complete, sacrificial love expressed on the cross, Jesus desired and expected his family to express itself as a family by constantly and sacrificially providing for one another. As a family, a local church body is to constantly remind its members that to be called the family of God requires that each member is concerned about the needs and spiritual welfare of every other member.

Bride of Christ. Another image utilized to describe the church in the New Testament is the bride of Christ. When the Apostle Paul described a healthy, godly perspective on the relationship between a husband and a wife, he referenced the loving relationship between Christ and the church. Paul called husbands to love their wives sacrificially in the same manner in which Christ loved the church, his bride. In writing to the Corinthian church, Paul described an intense love of Christ for the church as he actually is depicted as betrothing the church as his personal bride. More than just reluctant obedience, as the bride of Christ, Jesus expected his church to passionately desire to obey his commands in order to please him. The love of God is evident in the life of a believer when he or she obeys Christ's commands, and those commandments are no longer deemed as burdensome. As Christ's very own bride, the church is to be found faithful only to him and never swerving in allegiance and devotion.

Branches on a Vine. Nearing his imminent sacrifice upon the cross, Jesus emphasized that the church's function was to be viewed as branches on a vine. The church is never to mistake its identity with Jesus, but believers are always to view their role as an extension of Jesus. Jesus' image of the church serving as branches on a vine should cause believers to rely more completely on him for their life and power support. Only if Christ's disciples remained attached to the person of Jesus will they even be able to produce any fruit for the kingdom. Jesus exhorted his disciples to understand that apart from the life support of the vine, the branches could not do anything on their own. The branch is actually useless if it

removes its attachment to the vine. In this image of the church, Jesus emphasized that the only way the church could ever accomplish great tasks for the kingdom is if they constantly reminded one another concerning their dependancy upon Christ.

Body of Christ. Another image that Paul utilized to describe the church was that of the Body of Christ. Paul desired to show the Corinthians that all of the members of the body were gifted and they all had a specific role in the body. The imagery of the body of Christ should cause believers to recognize the need for one another. A mutuality exists between members of the body. Members understand that they encourage or hinder one another's growth. By emphasizing the church as serving in the role as the body of Christ, Paul celebrated the unified diversity represented in a local church. As Jesus' physical body was manifested during his personal ministry on earth, the church, serving as the body of Christ, is now his ministerial representation on earth.

The immense range of gifts represented within the church displayed the need for one another, but it also showed God's ingenuity concerning the differing types of gifts and special places within the body. The spiritual life of believers was never intended to be viewed solely in a personal context. As the body of Christ, believers are constantly to be mindful of the expected interdependency they have upon one another. Paul taught the Ephesian church that they were to rely expectantly on one another to be bold enough to speak the truth in love when one member strays from obedience. Within the body of Christ, the blood of Jesus has removed any blockades for admission and removed any stigma of preferential treatment. The body of Christ does not recognize the difference between nationality, race, or gender. The church is to view its members' roles as serving a specific function, and Christians are always to be mindful of their reliance on one another for spiritual maturation.

The Buildings. The authors of the New Testament also record different building imagery for the church. While they never viewed the church as a specific building, the authors did use buildings as illustrations to explain the theological implications of the church. As the church members construct the building structure, Paul reminded them that the church could be built on no other foundation than Jesus Christ. Peter described church members as living stones of a temple built upon the cornerstone, Jesus Christ. As his temple, the church should be aware that Jesus' presence is constantly among its members when the believers gather together. As they gather together, God expects them to offer spiritual sacrifices to God.

The "Perfect" Church

Now you know how the Bible describes a church; how do you go about picking between all these different churches? While you will not be able to find a perfect church, I truly hope that you can find a great one. When I counsel college students about committing to a church, I want to make sure they can say that the church is the perfect place to belong, to grow, and to serve.

Belong. You desperately need to find a church to which you can belong. Speaking theologically, you can't go to church since you are a part of the church. It is not a building; it is a body. You are a part of the Body of Christ, so when you find a church, you are simply committing to one section of the larger body.

Anne had transferred to the college in our town in the middle of her college career. She initiated meeting with me concerning church membership. She would only be in town for a couple of years, but she was feeling a prodding to join our church. The size of our church was such that not many would even recognize if she had not become a member, but she stated, "I don't want just to attend casually over these two years. I want to commit to this church so I can grow and give myself away."

I wish all Christians had that concept down. While you can attend a church and actually be involved in its ministry without signing a piece of paper, the absence of formal commitment always tends to lead people to pseudo-community. Without any commitment, it is easy for you to attend occasionally and to serve sporadically. When you join a church, you are indicating to that family that you belong to them and they belong to you. You want their help in your accountability. You want them to pray for you, to walk with you, and to serve with you. If all you ever do in college is church hop, you will miss out on the family of God that Jesus intends for all believers to possess.

Grow. Not only do you need to find a place to belong, but you also need to find the best place where you can grow. Just because a lot of people attend a church doesn't mean that people are growing. Crowds do not necessarily indicate discipleship.

Is the pastor committed to the Word of God? Do the messages attempt to change lives? Is there a strategy present for discipleship? Your involvement in a local church should produce nothing less than spiritual growth. While you play a huge role in how much biblical information you apply, a church should deliver biblical instruction in an attempt for your corresponding application.

I would also recommend that your plan for spiritual growth includes more than attentiveness during a sermon. In my experience, college students who grow the most are those who are involved in some type of small group experience tied to a local church. This extra step provides you with a chance to move past an informational sermon to a transformational message. In a small group setting, you are able to apply head knowledge into the different areas of your life.

Serve. Do not fall into the temptation of becoming a spiritual couch potato. If you have ever uttered the words concerning church, "I just didn't get that much out of it," you have totally missed the point. As a part of the church, you are meant to give yourself away. Its interesting that so many people want a church that solely supplies good information.

I had many friends in college who would come back from services and said, "I just wasn't fed today." When people make statements like that, they are referring to someone giving solid, "meaty" teaching. When Jesus talked about getting "fed," its very interesting to note that he spoke of doing the will of his Father as his food (John 4:34). He never equated spiritual nutrition with hearing the Word but rather doing the Word.

> If you have uttered the words concerning church, "I just didn't get much out of it," you have totally missed the point.

While you need to find a local church to which you can belong and where you can grow, you must find a place to serve in ministry. While you may not feel that you have that much to contribute, you must understand that Christ has gifted you specifically to meet a need in a local church as a member of the Body of Christ.

If you have ever played the game Jenga, you understand the importance of each part. When you first begin, removing one piece from the Jenga board doesn't shake the whole structure, but the more you remove, the more unstable the structure becomes. If you neglect getting involved in a local church, it may not shake the structure with just your absence, but what about when others drop out too? If God has wired you in a particular way, you must understand that God has a particular place to get you involved within the ministry of a local church.

Church Shopping

Where do you start? I would recommend that you put a timetable on when you are going to choose a church to commit yourself to while you are in college. Commit to visit churches for no more than two months. Decide that by the end of the timetable that you will commit yourself to that congregation and get deeply involved in the life of that church.

First, in identifying what churches to visit, I would locate Christian leaders on your campus that truly love Jesus and find out to which churches they belong. Don't ask lukewarm Christians. Find out those students who obviously love Jesus and follow them to church this week. Normally, students who care about the Bride of Christ have already undergone the process of finding a church, and you can benefit from their research and decision.

Second, visit some of those different churches. Don't go into worship with your radar on looking for flaws. Go in prepared to meet with God. As you engage him and worship with those believers, God will reveal certain things to you without your scrutinized efforts.

Third, once you have visited churches, ask yourself if that was a family to which you could belong, grow, and serve. Could you see yourself belonging to that family more than sitting next to them through an hour-long service? Could the leadership of that church challenge your spiritual growth? Is there a place in that church where you could serve?

Fourth, seek God about your decision. Ask God to help reveal to your heart where he is moving. Seek peace about his direction and your placement. As you pray about that decision, get a copy of that church's belief statements. Investigate their theology and see if it matches the teachings of Scripture. You must feel confident about the church's biblical theology before you can truly get behind it. If a church's theology checks out, inquire of God through prayer whether or not this is the place to call home.

Fifth, don't replace a church for a campus ministry. While there are great campus ministries out there, nothing can replace the life of a local church. I have seen too many students immerse themselves solely in a parachurch organization during their time in college. Once they graduate, they don't know how to connect to a church because they replaced God's ideal with what should have been viewed as a supplement to spiritual growth.

Finally, commit yourself to that church body. Meet with one of the ministers and tell him that you want to commit yourself to his spiritual care (Heb. 13:17). Explain to him your intention of being the church for the time that you are in college, and watch what God can do among you through the life of a local church.

I love the local church because Jesus does. He has ordained the church to be the instrument through which he reaches the world, and if you want truly desire to grow in college, the local church is essential to your development.

Group Questions
Chapter 7: **the Church Hop**
Don't merely attend church, be the church.

1. How do people normally determine whether or not a specific church is quality?

2. Concerning your own church involvement, how would you classify yourself? Do you neglect, hop, spectate, or belong?

3. What do you miss out on if all you do is attend church services?

4. Read Hebrews 10:24-25. In order to have these types of relationships within a local church, what will you have to change?

5. What should your next step be concerning being the church?

Pray that you stop going to church and start becoming the church. Pray that God reveal to you a group of people to whom you need to belong.

the **Outreach**

Casual Christianity causes casualties.

An inevitable part of college life is the summer job. Every May, college students everywhere start trying to find the best place of employment. So when it came to finding myself a summer job, I had worked enough places that helped steer me away from certain employment possibilities.

My first job in high school was blowing things up. I'm serious. My friend and I went to construction sites after the crew was finished building a house, and we would clean up the entire site by building a huge pile of trash and then we would explode the pile. We built the pile far away from the house because we were never sure exactly what type or how many chemicals were in the various containers at the bottom of the pile. Due to the volatile possibilities, we would have to propel a flame into the pile as we desperately ran for our lives. This summer job was the greatest way to earn money for a teenager – provided I survived the whole ordeal.

In the wintertime, I needed another job. My sister had worked at a shoe store, and she got me a job there. I would tell people that I worked at a women's shoe store, which was partially true. In shoe stores, ninety-nine percent of the inventory is for women, and then there exist a couple of tennis shoes and penny loafers in the corner for men. I had only one rule when I went in for this job: I wasn't going to touch anyone's feet. Luckily, they never made me. Placing shoes on women's feet that I didn't know made me feel cheap and used. I just couldn't handle it.

During Christmas break, I worked as a waiter for a country club in town. My roommate cooked in the back, and I would take the food out on the floor. We worked with two dishwashers. One was named Batman who kept all the extra food for his pit bulls. The other dishwasher was a blind man named Glenn who played keyboards in a band called "The Great White Buffalo." I only wish I was creative enough to make this stuff up.

Selecting a summer job was extremely important. While many of my friends decided to be lifeguards, amusement park workers, or interns at a really fun place to work, I chose a different path. I let my roommate talk me into working on an assembly line.

You haven't experienced the working world until you have worked on an assembly line. I made the bottom sashes of skylights all summer long. I stood in the same spot my entire shift. It was too loud to talk to anyone. You couldn't do anything different because you had to meet quota of bottom sashes everyday. The only excitement I got was when I dozed off and accidentally put a screw into my hand and had to go to the med cabinet.

I worked with some great people there. I loved getting to hang out with them at lunchtime where we could actually talk once the machines were turned off, but it didn't take me too long to notice that I also worked with some people who weren't putting Jesus as the center of their lives either. For example, when I accidentally put that screw into my hand and headed to the med cabinet, a lady grabbed my hand and told me not to go in there. When I told her I was bleeding and feeling a little dizzy, she told me that she didn't care. If our entire plant made it two more days without an injury, we all got bonuses. She wanted her bonus, and she was built like a linebacker and could have made a light snack out of me.

Needless to say, we got our bonuses, and I bled all day.

However, when I got to know these fellow workers, some interesting information was presented. I watched the ones who would quickly offer up a silent blessing when no one was looking, or so they thought. I watched the ones who felt uncomfortable because of the dirty jokes but failed at their attempts to refrain from laughing. As I spent more time with these people, I realized that some of them were very far off from God.

One guy in particular named Tony really began to grab my heart. I felt as if God was telling me that I needed to talk to him about my faith in Christ, but I was scared to death. I had great excuses though: 1) the machines are too loud to hear anything, 2) our breaks aren't long enough to get into a deep conversation, and 3) one of my foundational evangelistic principles is to never have a spiritual dialogue with a man who has a drill in his hands.

The more I made excuses to God, the more God impressed him on my heart. I would pray for him. I would think about how to start the conversation, but days went by, and I never initiated the conversation.

So God decided to initiate it himself.

One day as I was working on the loudest machine in our section, Tony came up and started talking to me. I couldn't hear a word he was saying, and after yelling at him to repeat it, I thought I heard him say, "Have you ate yet?"

I yelled back, "Playa, I ain't ate yet, it's only 10:00!"

He yelled back, and I finally heard him question me, "No, I said, are you saved?"

I responded, "Yeah, I'm saved. Are you?"

"No," he replied. And then he just walked back to his station like nothing ever happened.

I ran after him and implored him what caused him to ask me that, and he really did not have a definitive answer. He just wanted to know. Over lunch that day, we began to talk about my relationship with Christ. He was concerned about what he could still get away with in the personal pleasure department if he became a Christian, and he honestly responded that he didn't think he could stop sleeping around and partying with the substances he loved in order to follow Christ and live a holy life.

We continued to talk over the summer. To my knowledge, Tony has not become a Christian yet, but I still pray for him. And when I think about him, I also pray for me because I am so deeply embarrassed that someone had to ask me about the greatest thing in my life.

I am so ashamed that someone had to drag out of me whether or not my life has been transformed due to a relationship with Jesus. As I talked to Tony about Christ, I already felt defeated because I wondered if he could ever grasp that Christianity meant anything to me if I was not the one initiating the conversation with him.

Too Casual

That episode in college made me realize something: casual Christianity causes casualties. When we are casual about our Christianity, when we are apathetic about others' spiritual stages, that indifference causes casualties. If you are going to believe the Bible and hold that there is no way to a relationship with God outside of a saving encounter with Jesus (John 14:6), you cannot be casual about that. If we honestly lived like we said we believed as Christians, we would not be casual about the things that determined eternity.

I can't think of many items in the Christian life that cause more shame in the hearts of believers than the area of personal evangelism. Every time I hear a message about evangelism, an ambush of guilt just rushes over me. When I read in the Bible the commands to share the gospel, I make promises that last as long as when they are uttered. I pray for open doors, God delivers the opportunities, and I neglect them more often than not.

The fact of the matter is that I am simply too casual about other people's spirituality. I urgently want to be in the place in my life where I can say what Paul said when he claimed: "I am not ashamed of the gospel" (Rom. 1:16). And I want to love people enough that I will undergo personal uneasiness if it means telling them the changes that Jesus has done in my life. The area of the outreach, intentionally reaching out to someone who does not know Jesus in a personal way, is one of the items that you can give weight to Christ in your life at college.

2 Bad Evangelism Models

In college, I saw two extremes of the outreach. The first extreme was the Holy Roller. I went to a Christian college. I saw plenty of these Holy Rollers. Someone is a Holy Roller if he shares evangelistic information devoid of any love for the person. He loves to proclaim pre-packaged spiritual presentations without any attention to the person to whom he is conversing. He is the kind of person who can make snide, careless comments about the possibility of others' eternal separation from God and not even blink an eye. He has an arsenal of intense gospel tracts armed with flames, pitchforks, and demons (oh my!) ready to drop them off to every waiter accompanied with a lame tip.

The second extreme was the Silent Witness. The Silent Witness seems to be an oxymoron, but those that hold to this evangelistic model do not think so. This person honestly hopes that by just living a "good" Christian life, people will notice their uniqueness, and they will be questioned concerning "What's different with you?" Rarely, does this transaction take place. But for the sake of not "turning anyone off," the Silent Witnesses never get intentional about sharing their faith.

Somewhere in between these two dangerous models has to be a healthy medium. If you really are concerned about another's relationship with Jesus, then you must care about finding a balanced approach of being both intentional and relational. In my experience, I believe that more college students are Silent Witnesses than Holy Rollers. In fact, many students decided to go the silent route due to a bad experience with a Holy Roller.

But if you really do believe in the reality of eternity, and you believe that Jesus' words are true, you have to begin to shake your apathy and immobility, and you must decide to do something about other people's spiritual conditions. If casual Christianity truly causes casualties, then we must be concerned about our outreach.

It Starts with Prayer

Paul spoke concerning the specifics of the outreach to the church in Colossae. As a missionary, Paul was constantly around people who needed to hear about Christianity desperately. In your mind, you might think of a missionary who wears weird clothes and eats weird food living in a weird place, but can you think of a greater mission field than the college campus where you study?

You are currently living in a place that is full of people who have never heard about Christ clearly or seen Christianity portrayed adequately. You are the missionary. For those of you on the traditional college campus, you probably have many different religions represented. For those of you on Christian college campuses, don't assume that everyone is a Christian because they have simply been exposed to Christianity.

Paul's model for missional living is essential to how you can be the salt and the light on your campus (Matt. 5:13-16). His approach is not casual, but it is effective. When Paul wrote to this church, he gave some helpful tips for those trying to live life with an intentional outreach in mind. He showed them that both the talk and the walk are important when it comes to sharing one's faith.

First, he asked them to pray for him and his outreaching buddies that God would open up a door for God's message to be delivered to those that are around them (Co. 4:3). Paul was not afraid to talk about Jesus by any means. In fact, he often was beaten, threatened, and a whole bunch of other things because of his inability to keep his mouth shut about Jesus (2 Cor. 11:23-28). But he still asked for these Colossian Christians to pray that God would open doors. Casual Christianity doesn't open its mouth, but intentional Christianity decides to ask for doors to be opened in order to speak when those opportunities present themselves.

When was the last time that you asked God to open up a door for you to share what Christ has done in your life with someone? I'll give you a warning: he will open the door! He keeps his promises. God isn't like us; he doesn't lie (Num. 23:19). So if God's Word tells us to pray for open doors, then if you pray for them, they will swing open widely. If you honestly want to share, then stop even right now as you read this paragraph, and pray: "God, will you please open a door today for me to outreach to someone who needs you." I'll wait.

Secondly, Paul asked them that they pray for his clarity as he shared. That petition should reassure us greatly. The Apostle Paul, who refuted tons of brilliant people with the truth of the gospel, asked for others to pray that he portray Christ clearly. I know that I have personally struggled with the feelings of inadequacy when it comes to sharing Christ, but I rarely ask those around me to pray for me that I present him clearly. I would think that Paul would tell these Christians, "Get ready because we are going to holy roll our way through these people with our theological arguments," but he didn't. He asked for other believers to pray for him.

This prayer request is one of the reasons you need a good small group. If you regularly meet with a group of people whose sole purpose is to encourage you to love and good deeds (Heb. 10:24), you probably pray for each other or at least collect prayer requests together. Christians love to share prayer requests. Even if people haven't prayed about the situation themselves, we love to give prayer requests. Sometimes I think gossip is disguised in prayer requests. Sometimes I think attempts to get attention are disguised by prayer requests. But rarely do I ever hear people make a prayer request that God open up doors for them to share their faith and that they share the faith clearly.

Think about it for a moment. The last time you were in a meeting with people and you were sharing prayer requests, what did you hear? You probably made a list of someone who has a major test this week, a sick great-aunt, a friend's boyfriend's sister's friend that broke her pinky finger, a stressful week, a need for a new job, and an unspoken. Those requests are all valid, and I think it is beautiful that we can share those needs with one another. My problem with most prayer times is that nobody actually prays for the things requested and most requests are centered on our comfort rather than God's Kingdom.

What would happen on your campus if a group of believers started making evangelistic prayers a regular item in your meetings?

I do pray for pinky fingers and stressful weeks and new jobs. But I pray that in the middle of recovery of a broken pinky finger, God will challenge that person to live a life more faithful to Jesus than ever before. I pray that a person will have eyes during their stressful week to notice the needs of others whose lives are characterized by stress that would make ours seem trivial. I pray that God send someone to a new job in which he can share the gospel in such a meaningful way that the new place of employment will have continual spiritual conversations due to that person's arrival.

What would happen on your campus if your small group or large group of assembled believers started making evangelistic prayers a regular item in your meetings? What if we exalted Jesus to the place of being able to answer prayers outside of our personal needs or preferences, and we started praying that his Kingdom advance on our campuses? Paul prayed for that. You should pray for that too.

The next time you are in your small group, your dorm Bible study, or your college Sunday school class, why don't you ask for prayer that God open up doors for you to witness? Cindy will ask that you pray for her paper in which she procrastinated. Rick will ask that you pray for his friend's mom's second cousin-twice-removed who had a tree limb scratch her car. And you ask that God open up doors for you to share your faith clearly, and ask it the following week. And then when the leader asks for someone to pray and there is that awkward silence because everyone is to embarrassed to pray (don't even get me started on this one), step up and pray for every thing that was mentioned. But pray for every request with the Kingdom in mind. I think a campus has yet to see what would happen if a group of people really started praying for the gospel to advance through every dorm of their campus.

The Walk: How to Live

After Paul asked them to pray for him, he was also concerned with the walk part of the outreach. He challenges these Colossian Christians to live lives conducted in a wise way aware that "outsiders" are watching (Col. 4:5). Paul understood that if we are saying something that contradicts the way that we live, it displays a distorted, ambiguous message. We must backup our message with holy lives.

It's like naming a dog "Stay" and yelling at him, "Come here, Stay. Stay, come here." It confuses the dog to a place of anxious hysteria. It's a mixed message. So is the Christian guy who tells his friend to change his life, but he hasn't changed his own yet. "Change your life, be just like me. Be just like me, change your life." There is a huge problem when there is no difference. You have to live wisely.

The outreach is so important to your spiritual development, but you will more than likely fail at it unless you have a good entourage in place. You can easily reach out to people if the people closest to you are people who are closest to God (see chapter three). If your best friends are people that are far from God and you are trying to bring them closer to God, you stand little chance for survival. But once you have the close group of encouragers, you have a group of people that you can reach out to and still make sure you're safe because of your entourage.

When I was in college, our room occasionally got messy. That's actually a bit of an understatement. It was hard to navigate through our tiny dorm room due to the piles of clothes, trash, and collections of random junk that people would just drop off in my room. It was hard to get around during the day, but it was nearly impossible at night.

If I was coming in late and my roommate was asleep, or if I had to go to the bathroom in the middle of the night, I didn't want to awaken my roommate because he was grumpy when he woke up. So I would try to move to the desired location without turning on any lights. I constantly stepped on game controllers or ran into our hammock until I learned the value of points of reference. I established points of reference in our dorm room, so that when it was dark, I could find my way. If I could find the fan, then I knew I had about four steps to my desk. If I could find my desk, I could move along my bed to find the closet. If I found the closet, I could find the door handle to the bathroom. When I established points of reference, it was easy to move confidently through the dark.

Your entourage should be your points of reference moving through dark places. If the closest people to you are people that are closest to God, you bring them in on the process of the outreach. As you build relationships with people apart from a relationship with Jesus, they are points of reference for you along the way. They are present to tell you when you getting close to a place that could hurt you. If you have this group, you are able to intentionally outreach but stay committed to Christ in the process.

I've witnessed so many college students attempt to be a "good influence" on people who in the end brought about spiritual disaster. So many Christians, on what seem to be good intentions, outreach to someone that they like hanging out with but who lives a little looser than they. The problem occurs when the one being outreached is more successful in his mission of bringing you down than you are of bringing him up.

You may not have thought about this concept, but people whom you are attempting to convert are also in the process of converting you. If you are developing a friendship with someone who is not currently following Christ, he might seem curious behind some of your stands on certain issues. He might think that it is odd that you don't do some certain things and other things you make a habit. He might even become interested in what you say about Jesus, but if he doesn't want to adjust his life to match up with the claims of the Bible, he only has one option: convert you.

If he is successful to bringing you down to how he lives, not only does he no longer have to worry about someone trying to change him, but he now has a great excuse of why he doesn't need to become a Christian: because the Christian to whom he is the closest lives exactly the way he does. This type of defeated outreach does not have a void spiritual impact; it impacts the person in a negative way. In fact, it hurts other people's attempts to reach them.

Paul warned to live wisely among people to whom we are outreaching. He also told us always to be wise with how we used our time with those people (Col. 4:5). It is wise to use that time to get to know that person, to make that person feel comfortable with you. It is wise to open up to that person and to befriend him. But if you never do the wisest thing – intentionally share with him concerning a relationship with Christ – what real benefit are you doing him anyway?

The Talk: How to Speak

Paul continues on to say that your speech should be gracious always being aware of exactly what to say to each specific person (Col. 4:6). To know how to respond to each specific person, you need to truly know each specific person, and it has always intrigued me that he said we are to respond to people. We evaluate where they are spiritually by what they say, and we use our experiences, our knowledge, our own relationship with the Lord to respond to them.

I served a summer in St. Louis working for a Christian camp called M-Fuge while I was in college. While I was there, the Holy Spirit was really dealing with me concerning my apathetic state concerning other people's salvation. I remember praying while I was driving a van through St. Louis. I just confessed to God how inadequate I felt about verbally sharing my faith with other people.

I've never heard an audible voice of God. Sometimes I wish that I had so that I could be clear concerning direction. Other times, I believe that if I really heard his voice, I would be terribly petrified and peaceful all at the same time. That day wasn't an exception. I didn't hear the voice of God, but I felt the Holy Spirit speaking to my heart and asking me this question: "What is so hard about bragging on me?"

All the outreach consists of is bragging lavishly on God.

I can do that. I'm not the best when it comes to developing theological arguments concerning the existence of God, but the reality is that not many people are arguing that anymore. I'm not the greatest Bible scholar in the world, and someone could probably stump me on some philosophical question, but there is one thing that no one can ever argue with me about: Jesus changed my life.

And Jesus changed your life. No matter how much someone may not like the fact that he did, he cannot argue with a transformed life. He can resort to arguments, but he can't argue with results. They can argue about facts until eternity arrives, but they are unable to negate what Jesus has done in you.

> He can resort to arguments, but he can't argue with results. No one can argue with the fact that Jesus changed your life.

That is what you are called to proclaim. You are to respond to each person wisely with the truth of what Jesus has done in your life. It's not prepackaged. It's never the same. But it's always Jesus. In every conversation, you try to find a way to get to Christ.

When the girl in class is bummed because her parents are getting a divorce, you talk about how Christ brought you through when your parents split. When your roommate won't go to church with you because of some hypocrites he knows, you confess your own hypocritical nature and why that reality is why we all need Jesus. When your co-worker has doubts if Jesus really loves her, you tell her your story of how you came to grips with the marvelous love of Christ.

Just Can't Help It

The open doors come from everywhere. If you begin to pray and ask God for them, they are going to be opening everywhere. But will your life be ready for the scrutiny that could come with those open doors? Are your prepared to make the most of every opportunity to respond to people about the gospel? Do you have enough material to brag on Jesus in every situation you come into?

Peter did. In fact, right after Jesus was taken into heaven and the Holy Spirit fell upon the disciples in such an amazing way that all people heard the gospel in their own language, Peter and the other disciples were threatened to stop talking about Jesus. Peter listened to the threats that he knew could possibly be backed up by stoning, imprisonment, or death, and he responded that it was simply impossible for them to stop talking about what they had experienced (Acts. 4:19-20).

He understood if they wanted to kill him for talking about Jesus. If what he was saying was truth, the crowd was going to have to turn their lives upsides down to follow Christ. For Peter, it wasn't a matter of life or death. He was simply unable to stop talking about Jesus. Do what they must, but he was unable to stop bragging about Jesus. He used to be stubborn, but now he was obedient. He used to be a coward, but now he was courageous. He used to be condemned, but now he was forgiven, and it was all because of Jesus.

That is what you are called to do. Regardless of how people respond, you are called to brag on Jesus. You tell people what he has done for you. You tell people about how he turned your life upside down, and then tell them that he can change their lives too.

Group Questions
Chapter 8: the Outreach
Casual Christianity causes casualties.

1. Would you consider yourself a Holy Roller or more of a Silent Witness? Why?

2. What inadequacies do you possess concerning sharing your faith with another person?

3. What areas in your life would you say that your walk does not match up with your talk?

4. Who are the people that God has placed in your life that need to hear the gospel?

5. Read 1 Thess. 2:8. While the goal is to present the gospel, which steps must you take now to start the process with the people you just mentioned?

Pray that God opens doors wide open for you to share his gospel. Pray that when he does open them, you will be willing to walk through them.

the Influencers

It's difficult to impact a world that's influencing you.

After my sophomore year in college, a few of my college buddies and I served for a couple of weeks on the mission field in South Asia. I remembered getting a yellow sheet at a BCM conference that had a list of all the different mission projects that were available for college students the coming summer. As I read through the job list, there was one specific project that caught my attention: Jesus film distribution on bikes in the mountains of a closed country. I recruited some friends and traveled there that summer. While we were there, we were amazed to see the beautiful countryside, we loved the ethnic food, but we really were overwhelmed at all that God did among us.

We stayed in one city for a couple of nights that had an outdoors basketball stadium surrounded by many restaurants and shops. In this section of the country, not only were we the only Americans that most of these people had ever seen in person, but also we were the tallest people they had ever seen. When we walked out to the basketball court, you should have seen the fear in their eyes. As an athletically challenged individual, I felt so empowered to finally have people fear me in an athletic environment.

We played some of the locals there, and to say we dominated would be an understatement. Now granted we still couldn't shoot that well, but we could always out rebound them. I just stood under the basket with my arms up and would dish it out back to the top until someone would finally score. It was incredible. We were legends. People would walk by us in the streets and call us names. I didn't know what they were saying at first, but I did recognize that a certain phrase was consistent. I finally asked our translator, and he said that the people were calling us the "great white giants."

The following day, the great white giants and I were finishing our trek down the mountain, and we entered the hotel lobby where the hotel manager said that a group of men were waiting for us at the basketball court and wanted to challenge us to a game. We had just finished walking miles up and down the mountain, and all we had was our hiking boots. We ate our meal, and in defense of our dynasty with a run of one day, we had to show up.

When we were walking down the street, we noticed something unusual. As we approached the stadium, a loud sound emerged above the noise of the city streets. We turned the corner and walked into the stadium, and in the stadium, we saw hundreds of locals standing on their feet cheering in anticipation of the upcoming game. All these people had shown up to see the great white giants play against their most qualified team to challenge the Americans. Across the court, we saw the largest guys this country had to offer. We do believe that this group of Asian Goliaths were this country's Olympic qualifying team, and we had just entered into an international competition with the reputation of the United States of America on the line. For the sake of the red, white, and blue, we had to represent.

And we did represent — very poorly. The score was pitiful. These guys looked as if they were playing a bunch of preschoolers. Besides cheering loudly for their team, the crowd did give us courtesy cheers when my roommate, Freaky P., would fall or act crazy trying to trick the other players. Words could never express how poorly we did. The nationals cheered for us to be courteous, but the great white giants ruined the name of our country for a few hundred individuals that night.

What was so ironic is that we never thought we were good basketball players until the night before that game. When we were pitted against a rag-tag group of shorter amateurs, we felt as if we were basketball stars. Once we played against guys who really owned the game, we realized how far off the mark we were when it came to basketball.

In fact, that's just like my spiritual life particularly in the area of worldliness. I tend to look at the shape of our world and the morals of people who aren't following Jesus and think that I am a pretty good guy. I look around at how blatantly sinful other people are, and my "respectable" and "quiet" sins don't seem as severe, and gradually I just get complacent. I look at other people's standard of holiness, and think I am doing pretty good, but when I go against the holiness prescribed in God's Word and seen in God's character, I see how horrible I am. When I pit myself against the holiness of God, I see how much further I still have to go.

My fear is that many collegiate Christians attempt holiness like we attempted basketball that night. Compared to the rest of your university, your holiness rightly deserves saint status. You are the Mother Theresa of the dorm just because you maintain some type of self-control in your living. You are the spiritual "great white giants." Even if you are "better" than other college students around you, are you holy when you compare yourself to God's standards?

When you pit yourself against a holy, righteous God, do you still find yourself holy? When Isaiah the prophet came into contact with God, his proper response was devastation. In the midst of God's immense holiness, Isaiah rightly responded that he didn't deserve to be there because he was sinful and he lived among a culture of people who were sinful (Isa. 6:5).

His scenario is similar to ours. We acknowledge the fact that we live in a godless culture. You might attend a university that mocks God and mocks godly living. Maybe you are surrounded by people who only call upon God when life's worries have overwhelmed them. We readily admit that we live on a campus or in a nation that does not fear God anymore.

What about you? Could you say, like Isaiah, that you are ruined in the presence of a holy God due to your unrighteous waywardness? My

> But even if you are "better" than other college students around you, are you holy when you compare yourself to God's standards?

hunch is that if you are reading this book, you actually don't think of yourself as that bad anymore.   Sure you know you have some sinful tendencies, but when you compare yourself to other students your age, you might view yourself as squeaky clean, but our standard is not other students. Our standard is God. For his word says to be holy because he is holy (1 Pet. 1:16).

Not of the World

In order to give Jesus weight in the area of those influencers in your life, you must beware of worldliness. I knew that I was to be in the world but not of the world, but I never could find a healthy balance of what that practically looked like on my college campus. No matter how much I tried to deny it, the culture around me was impacting me. Sociology was diluting my theology. Even on a Christian campus, I found myself tolerating certain things that at one time I knew weren't edifying. The more and more I allowed certain influencers closer to me, the more I found myself being shaped by the values of my culture.

In John 17, Jesus is teaching his disciples a pretty intense lesson. Aware that his crucifixion is near, he reminds his disciples that he is about to depart from them.   To prepare them for life without the physical presence of Jesus near them, he shares these words: "I do not ask you to take them out of the world, but to keep them from the evil one. They are not of the world, even as I am not of the world" (John 17:15-16).

Some Christians over the years have gotten this idea messed up. They think that to steer clear from worldliness, they need to detach themselves from the world.   By building isolated communities or removing any possible influential mediums from homes or joining a monastery, many people have attempted to live detached from the world.

Actually, Christ didn't call us to detach from the world. How can we impact a world if we are detached from it? Jesus asked his Father to keep the disciples in the world, but he asked for protection from the evil of the world. His statement led to a popular coined phrase today that Christians are to be in the world but not of the world.

Recently, many Christian leaders are advocating for a removal of Christians from godless environments. I don't think that was Jesus' intention at all. Christ would desire that we live in the world but remain unscathed by the world. His prayer is that we could live in the middle of a worldly culture and still persevere by loving Jesus.

Before you skip this chapter for fear that I am going to tell you that your only media intake should be Southern Gospel and VeggieTales, hang with me. I am not going to tell you what media you should allow to influence you, but I do want to challenge you. Ignoring some honest critique will not help you. If there is nothing wrong with the influencers in your life, then you should not have to worry about any significant life changes.

If there are problems with what you are allowing to shape your morals, then you need to change some habits before they change you. I want to help establish some principles in which you can give Christ glory in your cultural intake. By looking at some scriptural passages, I hope to at least provide you with some gauges to judge what you allow close enough to impact you. To do an honest evaluation, you need to see if any influencers in your life are causing you to be calloused, compromised, or conformed.

 I started playing guitar my eighth grade year. I almost quit two weeks after my first lesson. Honestly, I wanted to play the guitar more than anything. My air guitar moves were getting better by the day, but I earnestly desired to add an actual instrument to my routine so that I could improve my audience from my bathroom mirror to some real people.

The reason I wanted to quit is that learning to play the guitar hurts. To make a decent, resonant sound on a guitar, you have to press the strings down very firmly. After a couple of weeks of practicing, the slightest touch to those strings sent my fingers wailing in pain. My guitar teacher informed me that if I could just persevere through those hard moments, one day I would develop calluses on my fingertips. Calluses are hardened parts on your skin that develop on your fingertips when frequent friction is applied. If I could develop calluses, I wouldn't feel the pain anymore. I can remember a time when playing the guitar finally stopped hurting. One day, my practice wasn't laborious anymore because I could no longer feel the pain. The friction was still there, but I had gotten desensitized to its painful reality.

In Ephesians, Paul warned those Christians about developing callused hearts which leads to ungodly living. He stated that the way that they lived started as a matter of the heart. Paul worried that these Christians would turn from Christ "due to their hardness of heart. They have become callus and have given themselves up to sensuality, greedy to practice every kind of impurity" (Eph. 4:18-20).

In the same way that calluses on my fingers removed the sting from guitar strings, calluses on our hearts can remove the sting associated when a Christian sins. The more I am around unhealthy influencers, the more callus my heart becomes. When once I could spot the vileness of sin a mile off, overtime I become desensitized to its destructive ploys. I start viewing certain sinful media presentations as funny or cute. I begin to accept certain unhealthy cultural phenomenon as natural, and before I know it, my heart is desensitized and my attempts at holiness wane in the process.

I have formulated a couple of tests to determine if I have gotten callused. You know you have become callused when a friend asks you how a movie was, and you have to reply, "It wasn't that bad. It only had a few cuss words in it." Busted. If you have to qualify a movie or music based upon the minimal amount of unedifying material, you have become callused. What I have found is that normally there was actually more inappropriate stuff in there than I admitted or even recognized; I just have gotten so desensitized to it that I didn't acknowledge its presence. When a movie only has a few inappropriate elements, most collegiate Christians rejoice that they don't feel as guilty to enjoy that flick. In an attempt to find the lesser of the evils, we can easily put our stamp of approval on things that honestly are not Christ-honoring.

Another simple test: would you watch that movie, listen to that song, or post on that site if your pastor was in the room with you? If you would feel uncomfortable with that scenario, you may have become callused. I was talking with a couple of students once at our church who started to sing a particular song, and then all of a sudden, they started blushing and said they couldn't finish the song. When I inquired why, they said they would feel awkward to utter the upcoming words around me.

I asked, "Are you uncomfortable to acknowledge that around one of your pastors or because its something you are embarrassed that you are listening to as a Christian?" I never received a response. The point is that if you feel awkward being influenced by some media medium around a minister, then you probably shouldn't be engaging with it anyway.

After you become callused to the culture, the next step is that you start compromising your own standards. While you once held to a certain desired level of holiness, you have now met somewhere in the middle between God's standards and the standards of the culture. This compromise is anything less than God's ideal.

The prophet Jeremiah told his culture that the people were in trouble because they were no longer ashamed when they sinned. He even states that the people around him had forgotten how to blush (Jer. 6:15). His culture was so immersed in sinful practices that they no longer felt a bit of shame for acting contrary to their spiritual heritage. These were the people of God, and they had begun to engage in things that should have been anything but characteristic of God's family.

When I was in college, the guys in my dorm had this discussion all the time. Since most of those guys were trying to live for Christ, nobody was doing any of the commonly accepted "worse" sins. We were just flirting with respectable sins. Respectable sins are those sins that church people really don't think are bad. Crude joking, coveting, lying, and other sins started to creep into behaviors, but since they weren't the really bad stuff, some of the guys never saw a need to change.

In one of our conversations, I remember that we were challenging each other on different issues. Some of these guys were getting ready to go help out at a church youth group, and I asked the question, "Will you tell those youth tonight at church that it is acceptable to live the way you are living?" The silence in the room revealed how we all felt. Nobody wanted to transgress against Christ, but we became aware of our tendencies to compromise in the shady areas.

Concerning worldliness, I still want to be uncomfortable with the things that make Jesus uncomfortable. I don't want to lose my ability to blush. I want to know that questionable things still show up on my radar, and I have enough unction to confront those gray areas. If friendship with this world means hostility towards God (James 4:4), then I want to make sure I don't compromise in my personal holiness or integrity.

Without a doubt, compromise comes in the form of our sin and our approval of others' sins. Christians don't openly condone sin, but when we make light of sinful actions in our world, we are not only accepting its reality but also we are celebrating its presence. Paul blasted those who not only sinned, but those who also gave approval to sinners (Rom. 1:32). In a compromised state, Christians enjoy the entertainment provided by transgression. If I enjoy a media piece that mocks biblical teaching, my morals have been compromised. If I find humor in the things that Christ died for, I am in a dangerous spot.

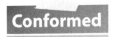

Conformed After someone is callused and compromised, the final step is to be conformed. In a very familiar passage, Paul instructs believers that their entire lives are to be an offering of worship to God. He then instructs believers to refrain from being "conformed to this world, but be transformed by the renewal of your mind" (Rom. 12:2). If you desire to live a life of worship offered to Jesus, you must realize that forces in this world exist to combat that reality from happening. This world is attempting to conform you to its standards rather than God's standards. A battle exists even if you aren't aware of its reality (Eph. 6:10-12). As the forces opposing God attempt to get you callused to the morals of this culture and compromising your own standards, the ultimate goal is to have you conform to the way of this world.

The test to see if you have been conformed is simple: are you being more conformed to the world, or is the world being more transformed by you? Is the world's standards chipping away at your resolve, or are you making advancements in this world for the Kingdom of God? If you seem to be losing ground in your stance to live godly, you are on the path to being conformed.

A Christian has conformed when he believes that climbing the corporate ladder of success is more beneficial to his future than answering in the positive to God's call on his life. A Christian young woman has conformed when she believes that she has to dress a certain way and perform a certain way to get a guy before she graduates college. A Christian young man has conformed when his perception of his girlfriend has diminished to a piece of attractive property rather than the inwardly beautiful daughter of God that she is.

Make no mistake: it's hard to impact a world that is influencing you. We were called to change this world not conform to it. Christ calls us to bring about his reign in the hearts of all people, but what happens when his own children reject his lordship over their own lives? When you have stopped seeking to see how you can be a change agent in this world because you have begun to love the things and the state of this world so much, you have already conformed, and its impossible to transform a world that's conforming you.

Only the Good Stuff

When I was in college, I worked at a summer youth camp called Centrifuge. That summer, I was staffed at Carson-Newman College for an amazing couple months of ministry. Our staff experienced long days. Early rising followed by constant moving, teaching, screaming, running, and all the rambunctious activities associated with youth camp led to some tired staffers. Sometimes you would have to choose between the luxury of eating a rushed meal or taking a quick nap.

In the more heated time of the summer, one of our staffers actually got pneumonia because of dehydration associated with the nonstop flow of camp. As a result of his hospitalization, all staffers were required to drink a large daily quota of water. We had to drink so much water that I would force my campers to take a couple of bathroom breaks during our hour-long Bible study.

I had never been a water drinker. A few months prior, I barely missed the cutoff time in the process of giving blood because of my carbonated veins. I never ever drank water. I hated the taste of it, but after a couple weeks of being hydrated by solely water, my body felt better than I could ever remember in my life. I never knew how good water tasted until I weaned myself off of carbonation. I never knew how good I could feel until I got all that mess out of my system.

I also never knew how good spiritually I could feel until I started filtering what influenced me. In college, I started weaning myself off of certain questionable, worldly material. I didn't remove myself from those influences by becoming a hermit. I just started allowing more positive stuff in than all the negative stuff. An important theological concept that Paul used a bunch is that whenever you take something away, you always need to put something in its place. As you put something off, you put something else on.

If I was watching a show on TV that started getting filthy, I changed channels. If some of my favorite tracks degraded women, I deleted them off of my computer. If somebody said that a movie wasn't "that bad," I just didn't even attempt it. I was surprised to realize how good I could feel once I got all that mess out of my system. My intake of God's Word, quality music and entertainment without the filth, and my accountability with my friends helped me get to a place spiritually that I didn't know I could go. Because I no longer allowed this world to transform me, I started putting stuff in my life that could help me transform the world.

Paul says that we should think on the things that are true, honorable, just, pure, lovely, commendable, excellent, and those things that are worthy of praise (Phil. 4:8). I found that there is a lot in this world that glorifies God, and I didn't have to be some ascetic weirdo to enjoy it. I just tried to get wiser with what I let influence me. Garbage in, garbage out. Good stuff in, good stuff out.

If we truly believe that we are at war in this world, we have to learn how to begin to take every thought that we have captive to the obedience of Christ (2 Cor. 10:3-5). Practically, that means that you can start filtering everything that influences you and determining whether or not that thing helps you grow in Christ or not. It is hard to impact a world that is influencing you. It is extremely difficult to transform a world that is conforming you. In order to give God glory in this area of your life, maybe you need to perform some serious self-evaluation to see what the things are that are truly influencing you.

Group Questions

Chapter 9: the Influencers

It's difficult to impact a world that's influencing you.

1. What is the standard of holiness on your campus?

2. How does what your campus considers as holy differ from what God considers as holy?

3. Are there areas in your life that you suspect you may have become callused to concerning unholiness?

4. Read 2 Corinthians 10:3-6. What does it practically mean to take every thought captive to the obedience of Christ?

5. Is there anything that you need to do right now in order to remove certain influencers from your life?

Pray that your heart not become so callused that you become comfortable with sin. Pray that God pinpoints ungodly influencers that may be prevalent in your life.

the **Budget**

*Some financial decisions will cost you more
than what you'll ever be able to afford.*

Money is tight in college. It's basically a nonexistent companion to struggling college students. Real cash is like a rumor that you hear about echoing throughout the halls of academia. Due to this reality, one of the most hilarious moments you will ever have in college will be surrounding your graduation day as your school officials prepare you for induction into official alumni status. Some schools share this moment through a talk in a meeting or through a publication. We received our talk at the end of graduation practice. Our school had a video presentation with accompanying forms to fill out in order to financially support our Alma Mater now that we were full-fledged alumni. They were asking money from some of the poorest people in America at that point. To clarify, most of us were not poor; we actually had negative funds. Many of my fellow graduates would be paying off that school for years to come and could not even begin to imagine how to invest money yet.

College graduates simply don't have a lot of money, but that fact doesn't mean that college students are not constantly trying to find ingenious ways to scrape around for money. You get mesmerized with so many great things that you think you need during your tenure at college. Due to that fact, many college students will make some ridiculous attempts to gain a little extra dough in order to buy the next best thing. Some of my friends made normal attempts to make money like getting a job, and then some of my cohorts tried some other unorthodox approaches.

One year, we had a resident assistant that wanted a new fishing rod. He liked to fish, and he was from deep in the back woods, so he decided to use his master key for the dorm and proceed to steal my buddy Kyle's fishing rod. When Kyle interrogated him about the fishing rod, the RA denied the allegation. He did offer to sell the rod to Kyle though. Kyle proceeded to pinpoint certain key functions of the rod proving that it was in fact his rod. Begrudgingly, the RA finally handed it over after much deliberation and replied, "Well, it's broke anyway."

Then there was my roommate, Freaky P. One day, he got a good lead that you could sell your blood platelets for money at a sketchy clinic downtown. Freaky P. was used to donating blood in which the normal routine would consist of his getting close to finishing, passing out, and then getting free food to revive him. I have a hunch that the food was part of his entire masterminded plan. Once this lead was confirmed, guys in my dorm would carpool to the clinic twice a week (that was the maximum number of times you could go), get their platelets extracted from their blood stream, and get a check cut for a little extra spending money.

Since the college I attended was nestled in the mountains, many students had mountain bikes. In fact, it was part of the getup for many. If you had a mountain bike, you were also mandated by the code of the mountain to wear Chaco's and shorts (even in the winter), and you had to sport some facial hair (even for the ladies). One of my friends wanted to be a part of this elite club. He had the outfit, but he didn't have the mountain bike. One of the mountain hippies told him that all he had to do was to take out a student loan, and he wouldn't have to pay on it until after he got out of college. So my buddy who had good scholarships took out a student loan for a thousand dollar mountain bike.

My friend was still paying the minimum payments on the bike years after college, and the bad thing was that he paid much more than a thousand dollars in the long run. He paid more than he anticipated because he was another victim to collegiate financial mistakes. These monetary blunders are some of the most dangerous in college, but since they don't appear to be urgent, they are rarely acknowledged. You can immediately see the consequences of academic procrastination, late-night binge drinking, or random hookups, but financial decisions are tricky. You can easily make a decision that immediately affects you in a good way that will paralyze you for years to come. Oftentimes, the immediate gratification causes you to overlook the consequences of bad financial decisions that might not catch up with you until literally years later.

Let me explain. When my friend purchased his mountain bike, he had immediate gratification. He was instantaneously riding bikes with the mountain hippies, and I was still playing Mario Kart inside the dorm. All he had to do was sign a form, they cut him a check, and he was riding a few days later. He didn't have to do anything concerning that loan for years.

The loan companies will loan you money at a low interest rate, but this purchase will cost you more than you think it will. It's honestly not about a mountain bike; it's about the need for a budget. It's about a choice to live wisely all the days of your life. It's the decision to choose contentment. It's about evaluating the ever-tempting American Dream and deciding the type of state in which you are going to live. In college, it is a hard decision to make.

I came close to applying for a student loan to purchase a mountain bike. I thought about getting a student loan on a bunch of different items when I was in college. It was this subtle temptation that I was reminded of every time I didn't have enough money for something I wanted. I always remembered that I had an option to get one of these loans or a credit card to whet my spending appetite. Maybe you have already taken out a student loan on a mountain bike. Maybe you are thinking about it, but I want to tell you something that I wish I had learned before going to college: some financial decisions will cost you more than what you'll ever be able to afford. If we take Jesus at his word, he told us that we could not serve both him and money (Lk. 16:13). Maybe our spending decisions are more of a spiritual decision than we ever imagined.

The Real Numbers

Our college group at my church was traveling to invest in some children at a missions project during the summer, and I was driving one of the vans full of students. I had just finished reading Dave Ramsey's, *The Total Money Makeover*, and I was befuddled at some of the stats I read. I polled those riding on the van and asked them how much of a stress factor was the area of finances in their lives. I was baffled. Some students already had student loans way into the tens of thousands of dollars. Accompanying that debt, many of them had accumulated thousands of dollars of credit card debt due to spending money on anything from Japanese food, Old Navy, and rent payments.

I investigated further. The average college graduate leaves college with approximately $20,000 in student loans and a staggering $4,000 in debt stemming from credit card purchases. Due to this immense debt, college students have a substantially less net worth than people their age fifteen to twenty years ago. More young adults are also postponing getting married and having children all because they are overwhelmed with their debt. When the Pew Research Center polled to determine the number one item causing stress in the lives of 18-25 year olds, they found that finances (debt, spending, etc.) was the number one answer for 30% of those polled topping relationships, family, education, career, and the uncertainty of their future. Over 80% of college students graduate with credit card debt even before they have been offered a job. Currently, 19% of Americans who file bankruptcy are college students.

I see the stress money brings on college students while they are still in school, but you are going to have to trust me when I say that you haven't seen anything yet when it comes to financial pressure. When you leave college, the stress becomes much worse when all those bills that were in the distant future abruptly become a present reality. I want to save you from making some mistakes that literally could cost you the rest of your life. Even if you don't see the need now, if you put into practice some of the following biblical principles into your finances, you will be able to give God glory through every spending decision you make.

**Don't Spend Money
You Don't Have**

The first major mistake that college students make concerning their finances is that they spend money that they simply don't have. From taking out student loans for major purchases to running up credit card bills for minor purchases here and there, college students are targeted to spend money that is not present. Ask yourself a question: why are financial institutions so eager to get college students to commit to their organization if college students are so broke? Why don't they seek out people with jobs and a good amount of money? In the long run, they make more money off of people like you who don't have the financial resources to settle debt quickly.

Many local banks offer free checking only to college students, but no other demographic in America receives this perk. They anticipate that when you get a free checking account with their company, you will then apply for a line of credit through them. They also anticipate that you are so busy with college life that you won't balance your bank account and subsequently use your debit card like crazy in order for them to make more money by charging you plenty of penalty fees.

Have you noticed the number of credit card companies on campus? The first week of school they offer freshmen free university t-shirts if they sign up for a free credit card. Don't doubt for a minute that they will not make their money back from you on that investment. Even if students only plan to use the credit cards for an emergency, the newest album from your favorite band quickly can become an "emergency."

It amazes me that university campuses even allow credit card companies the opportunity to rob their students. The reason your campus' administration allows their presence is that the university gets a good sum of money for these companies to invade your student body. I have worked with a campus that will not allow churches to post signs about a Bible study, but they encourage credit card companies to convert their students into addictive spenders with limitless credit.

Regardless of your campus's stance on credit card solicitation, you will be the one who decides whether or not you are going to make it a habit to spend money that you don't have. Taking out loans, charging all of your purchases, or borrowing money from someone all have the root that you feel compelled to spend money that isn't yours. You might have a legitimate financial need, but quite often you can get caught up in endlessly spending since you don't have to presently deal with your rising debt.

I have a rule about spending: unless it is a house, car, or education, I don't borrow money. I do not have a credit card. Once I got a job, I decided to save money for any spending that I needed to do, but I never borrowed money. I definitely never borrowed money from family because that leads to scrutiny on everything you own. I don't take out a loan for anything unless it is a legitimate need in one of those major areas.

Before you write me off as being un-American, understand that my reasoning is not solely logical. I got this tidbit of advice from the Bible. Solomon, one of the wealthiest men of all-time, wrote that rich people rule over poor people and that someone who borrows money from someone else has become that person's slave (Prov. 22:7). I would expect a wealthy person to encourage a borrowing mentality, but he warns against it because when you choose to use money that you presently don't have, you are the lender's slave until you pay it back.

Not only do you become slave to the lender when you borrow money or charge something on a credit card, but you also will have to pay much more for the purchased item due to the accumulating interest. The average $100 purchase for a student on a credit card will actually cost him so much more than a mere $100. If you already have a credit card or two, you have to begin to ask the question: do I truly need what I am purchasing on credit?

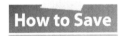

How to Save If you honestly don't desire to graduate from college with a tremendous amount of debt, have you ever thought how you could start saving money? Outside of student loans, the majority of the debt cases stem from purchases that I would consider luxury items. Most credit purchases are on non-essential items.

One major area in which college students throw their money away is in their eating out at countless restaurants. I admit that I'm a cheapskate when it comes to eating out. I love to go to a nice restaurant, but I would be content with eating sandwiches every night if it meant I could save money. I'm just weird that way. Also, the majority of educational plans provide a good meal plan. Many students decide to lower their meal plan or pay for it and never eat in the dining hall.

I have had this conversation many times concerning the nervous walk to the serving lines in many campuses' dining halls. I too have experienced the suspicions concerning Friday's entrees being created by a conglomeration of the week's leftovers. Every college student has partaken of some delicacy that made him or her run for the bathroom with speed that set your school's track record for the fifty-yard dash. Regardless of the quality, the food is cheap. You could probably eat better at Chili's every night of the week, but when your entire paycheck ends up missing due to eating out every night, you might want to reconsider your eating habits.

I admit it was unfair for me in college. I am not a picky eater. In my house, we were always taught to be grateful for what we had, but due to my experiences in overseas mission trips in college, I could and would eat anything and everything. Once you have eaten raw fish, pigtail, fried yellow jackets, and pickled chicken feet, Meatloaf Surprise in the school cafeteria doesn't raise that many flags anymore. It raises some flags, but not enough to keep me from eating it.

The only times I ate out in college was when my dorm would go to the cheap barbeque joint with questionable health ratings and when I would take my girlfriend out on the weekends. Besides those meals, I ate every meal in the cafeteria. Sure I would have liked to eat out more often, but when it came time that I needed to buy my girlfriend an engagement ring, I did not have to borrow money because I had been able to save since I learned how not to blow my money eating at expensive restaurants all the time.

 Another area that college students lose a whole lot of money is in their lodging. Dorm life in college is rightly characterized by cramped spaces and suffocating quarters. My bathroom at home was almost larger than my entire dorm room shared by two guys. If you choose to bypass dorm life and get an apartment or a rental house, your score on the popularity scale automatically increases by ten points because you now have *the* place to hang out. Unfortunately, you also have to put money down on something that will never belong to you.

I never learned about many of the areas of personal finances while I was in college. In fact, I wish they had made me take a class on finances in college because I was clueless by the time I graduated. When I went to buy my first home, I felt as if the bankers were speaking a different language due to the terminology that I was simply never taught. You are not going to have that excuse. You are about to receive possibly your first course in Real World Finances 101.

We'll start our education in the lodging department since we are on that subject. Let's say that you finished college and you wanted to purchase a $100,000 home. You had to take out the majority of that price on a mortgage loan ("mortgage" is the payment you make on a home). You have an incredible amount of interest (the money that the bank charges you for borrowing money from them) that you always pay on that home. In a few years, imagine you have paid off $10,000 on that home. You'll pay the bank much more than that due to interest, but the $10,000 you have paid off of the house's actual cost is money that will always be accredited to you. If you decided to sell that home, you will receive the $10,000 to put on your next home. Plus, your home is the one thing in life that actually makes you money. The price inflates or makes money while you live in it because the housing market is normally going up, unlike when you drive a car new off of the lot, it automatically loses thousands of dollars of value by the time you enter the main road.

If you rent an apartment or a house for $500 a month (which is a really good find), you will spend $10,000 on that home in twenty months. That means in just a little more than three semesters, you will have spent $10,000 on your lodging. Do you know what happens with that $10,000 when you leave that apartment? You will never see a dime of it again.

The apartment manager begins to look for another set of college students to pay $10,000 for another three semesters.

Realizing that most college students get a roommate or two or thirty-three to help out with these costs, it is still discouraging to realize that you are spending a good amount of money that you will never ever see again. Living on campus costs money as well, but it doesn't cost as much as living off-campus. Wouldn't it be discouraging to know that you spent $10,000 on living in a place temporarily when you could have been saving money for your future house?

Bad Spending Habits

Besides food and lodging, there are plenty of other spending temptations. Maybe you have the honest desire to dress like the most popular students on campus. You don't want to drive your mom's minivan when other students are driving sports cars. With the click of a "Buy" button, you can easily get all your favorite music on iTunes and simultaneously run up a bill of a hundred dollars. Ultimately we spend and borrow, and we begin to develop a method of spending that is self-destructive.

It is rare for a student to think about how to save money in college. The combination of freedom and access to credit cards leaves one numb to how much money he is actually spending. I don't think eating out or living off-campus is ungodly. I don't think it is a sin to purchase an iPod, an L. L. Bean jacket, or a Guitar Hero wireless controller, but I do think that unwise financial decisions will cost you more than what you ever can afford in the long run.

One of the passages that helped me out most during college was found in Philippians 4. Paul's confession of "I can do all things through Christ who strengthens me" (Phil. 4:13) is one of the most well-known and loved verses of the Bible. A good rule to use when reading the Bible is the importance of reading each passage in context. Whenever anyone quotes that verse, I normally inquire if they know what verse twelve states. Because verse twelve has a lot to do with how you spend your money and in the manner in which you will live. Paul stated that he had learned how to be content in all circumstances. He declared that "I have learned how to get along with humble means and how to live in prosperity; I have learned the secret of having abundance and suffering need; I can do all things through Christ who strengthens me" (Phil. 4:12-13).

Most people love to quote that Christ will give us strength for the hard situations which we encounter, but Paul was actually stating that he knew how to eat well and how to do without. He understood what it meant to live it up and how to live on a budget. He could do any of it, regardless of the circumstances, because Christ gave him the strength.

Can you? Could you eat at the cafeteria a whole bunch during your college career? Could you live in a dorm that should have been condemned when your parents went to school there? Through Christ's strength, could you learn to be content in order not to make unwise spending decisions that will drastically affect your future?

The only thing telling us we deserve better than what we are presently experiencing is pride. Selfishness causes us to be spoiled brats who demand everything we want. We see other people with the nicest cars because their dad makes more money. All the girls that you think are the prettiest have the best clothes money can buy. You want the new gaming system that your friend has because he got you hooked on it. Unfortunately, you simply don't have the money, and it is not fair.

Let's clarify: it's not fair to compare. Pride tells us we deserve more, and that we should have it better than other people. So if we deserve more, we will get more at whatever it costs. What is the answer to ease our extravagant, materialistic hearts? We need more money. That's why Paul told his apprentice, Timothy, that the love of money was the root of all kinds of evil (1 Tim. 6:10).

The more we indulge in what the world has to offer, the more attached we become to the things of this world. When I was personally struggling with the infection of greed in my life, I went to God in prayer. I was praying something fierce because I had bought into the lie that I deserved better than what I currently had. As I prayed and sought God's heart by reading the Bible, I came across a passage of

Selfishness causes us to be spoiled brats who demand everything we want.

Scripture that changed my heart on my living situation. Paul stated that godliness was a means of great gain when it was accompanied by contentment. He then stated, "We have brought nothing into this world, and we can not take anything out of it; if we have food and covering, with these we will be content" (1 Tim. 6:6-8).

I didn't like these verses too much upon reading them nearing graduation. I wasn't fond of them because Paul didn't clarify what type of condition the food and covering would be. He should have stated that we should be content when we live in the best, eat the best, and have the best. Instead, if he simply had anything to go in his mouth and anything to cover his head, he chose to be content.

The main reason I think God has instructions concerning greed, debt, and contentment, is that he wants you to experience the greatest gift when it comes to money: giving it away. If you are at the point where the only finances that you possess are what you can swipe with some plastic, I am not asking you to give to the local charity through charging it, but you do need to figure out how you can start giving your money away. God absolutely loves a cheerful giver (2 Cor. 9:6-7), because giving is one of the ways our hearts can become more like God's heart.

I read a lot of books about churches and the changing culture. Researchers and cultural analysts praise the young generations for their passion to make a difference in the world. Many church leaders state that previous generations saw church as solely about meeting their personal needs and not looking for those outside the church. They believe that your generation does not want to solely meet in a church building, but you want to be the church by going all over the world to reach out to those in need.

They also state about your generation that you are not concerned about putting your wallet where your feet are. Previous generations were very willing to invest money in a missions cause and hear about someone else doing it. The up and coming generations want to do something about it without putting any financial backing in it. God's heart is that both realities are present in the lives of believers. He wants you to give and to go. If you decide to wait to give until you have the adequate financial structure, you will never give.

Our view of money cannot change depending upon the amount we possess. If you have $100 to your name, you should approach that money the same way you would approach it if you were a millionaire. All of it belongs to God (Ps. 24:1). You can't take any of it with you (Ps. 49:16-20). If you make your life's pursuits about accumulating wealth, you will have lived for a pathetic goal that you may attain but you will never possess because it stays on this earth once you die.

If Jesus was correct that wherever your treasure is, there your heart will also be (Matt. 6:21), then you need to evaluate in what you are investing. K. P. Yohannan, president of the Gospel for Asia organization, stated that the average American spends more on dog food than they will spend supporting missions. Maybe you haven't been spending your money on dog food, but you might be amazed at how shallow your spending record looks like when you look at the needs of the world. How much money have you given to the needs of others compared to your personal desires?

Someone once challenged me by saying that he could tell a lot of my spiritual condition by looking at my checking account. When I was a college student, I could rarely find my checkbook, and so I just swept my debit card on the regular. If I was to print off a statement of my purchases in college, what percentage of the purchases was based on selfish desires in an attempt to procure luxury items? What percentage of my purchases was based upon a desire to expand God's Kingdom?

I really got challenged. I realized that I had been attending church all throughout college, but I was irregular about tithing. I guess I just thought since I did not possess a regular job, I was exempt in giving to God's work being carried out through the local church. I said I didn't have money, but I surely had enough to buy stuff that I wanted. Maybe it wasn't the fact that I didn't have money; I just was unwise in my spending.

The best reason to live on campus and eat in the cafeteria is not to be a tightwad, but it's to be a charitable giver. It's to be more like Christ. You will never have enough money. There will always be more that you could get if that is your earnest desire. If your heart is to be a steward who has been made rich through Jesus' poverty on earth (2 Cor. 8:9), and you want to give as much as you can to advance God's Kingdom rather than your own, you are in good shape. John Wesley once said, "Gain as much as you can, save as much as you can, give as much as you can."

So where do you start? First off, decide to make Jesus your one thing. You will never make two masters happy (Lk. 16:13). Take an hour every month and really sit down and look at how you spent money in the last month (you might be shocked). Stop spending money that you don't have. Start paying off debt before the major interest rates hit – you will be glad you did. Ruthlessly, eliminate the debt you have already accumulated. Spend wisely. Figure out how much you are going to give to others before you spend on yourself. Save some money. Trust not in the uncertainty of riches, but on God (1 Tim. 6:17-19) and learn to be content in any situation in which you find yourself (Phil. 4:12).

Group Questions

Chapter 10: the Budget

*Some financial decisions will cost you more
than what you'll ever be able to afford.*

1. Before you entered college, what type of financial advice had you received?

2. How can financial problems affect other areas in someone's life?

3. To whom does your money belong? How does your answer change your perspective on money?

4. Read 1 Timothy 6:6-8 and Philippians 4:12-13. What should a contented life look like?

5. What practical steps could you begin to take to manage the money entrusted to you in a God-honoring way?

Pray that God contents you. Thank him for his blessings and pray that you be a faithful steward with whatever amount he has given you.

the **Classroom**

Love the LORD your God will all your mind.

In high school, I never became an avid studier. When I started college, I anticipated maintaining the same amount of slack effort I had exerted in my high school studies and hopefully achieving the same results. Early on in my college career, I realized that changes were desperately needed concerning my study habits, or else great harm would fall upon me from the hands of my mother.

When I met with my advisor the summer before my freshman year, I had a tentative class list established in my mind. Some of the classes were non-negotionables. I had to take certain classes for my intended major. Concerning other class selections, I had some choices. When it came to the needed math credit, I asked the advisor to enroll me in a calculus course, but he signed me up for an intermediate algebra course. I began to educate this obviously uninformed counselor of my massive math skills and how I should take a calculus class due to the level of classes I had completed in high school.

My advisor replied, "Travis, let me explain something about college. You need one math course to graduate college. You can receive an easy 'A,' or you can struggle for a difficult 'A,' but an 'A' is an 'A.' Do you understand?"

I loved intermediate algebra. On the first day, we took a placement exam. Since I had taken many math courses in high school, I eased through that examination. The next class period, my professor informed me that I didn't have to come to class that semester if I didn't feel like it. College was starting out pretty good.

I can't say I had the warmest of affections for my biology course though. I applied the same amount of lackluster effort that I had utilized in the past, and for whatever reason, I was unable to receive the high grades that I anticipated. I found out that daydreaming in class, failing to read the textbook, and semi-cramming efforts the night before a test (while still attempting to partake of our dorm's slip and slide down the hall) unfortunately did not produce good grades. After my first semester, I realized that I was not going to be able to waltz carefree through college.

My sophomore year, something clicked inside of me. I was taking my first Greek course with a professor that had a reputation for more students dropping the course than finishing the course, and I pridefully thought to myself that I could make a light snack out of this man. Unfortunately, this professor intended to make a light snack out of me. My minimal efforts at cramming the night before the first exam were nowhere near adequate.

As I placed the test face down on my professor's desk, he slid a piece of paper across the desk towards me and stated, "I brought one of these for you. I thought you might need one." I picked up the piece of paper to realize that my gracious Greek professor was so thoughtful that he brought a course drop form for me to fill out upon completion of my exam. He was not joking. He laughed, but he was not joking. I don't know if it was the sweat on my brow as I walked to the desk or the massive amount of incomplete answers on my test that gave me away, but regardless, he was anticipating my giving up that fateful day.

As I told him that I didn't need the form, he asked me to reconsider. When I asked him why he was so insistent on my dropping the course, he replied, "I've seen ministry majors like you come and go. You are so wrapped up in doing ministry that you don't take seriously the preparation of ministry. Guys like you make spiritual excuses why you haven't done your homework. Do yourself a favor and fill this form out now because it only gets harder from here."

As I stormed out of that classroom that day, I was infuriated. I was not upset at his comment. I was upset because he was exactly right. I was not taking my studies seriously, and my grades could prove it. I made it my goal that day that I was going to make a believer out of him by the end of the semester. I was going to be a Greek scholar if it killed me, and it almost did.

With All Your Mind

When Jesus was asked to reveal the greatest commandment, he replied to those questioning, "You shall love the Lord your God with all your heart and with all your soul and with all your mind and with all your strength" (Mark 12:30). He also stated the second most important concerning loving one's neighbor as oneself (Mark 12:31). Both of these commands were a simple recitation of commands found in the Jewish law in the Book of Deuteronomy.

Many college students love these verses. This simple expression of Christian devotion unifies all of God's commands under the description to love God and to love others. If we can handle those two concepts, all the other commandments fall into their rightful place. Concerning the first command of loving God, many college students passionately quote this verse concerning worshiping God freely, serving others, or striving to grow spiritually. We love to love God with our heart, soul, and strength, but why don't we ever attempt to love the Lord our God will *all* of our mind?

God gave us capable minds to entertain grandiose thoughts of him, and we rarely ever try to grow more intelligent for the sake of Jesus. When I entered college, the only reason I wanted to get good grades was to impress certain people. If I didn't receive exemplary grades, I simply stated that I wasn't interested in that subject or that particular professor wasn't reasonable. During that semester, I investigated my life and realized that I was not loving God with all of my mind or even the majority of my mind.

I loved to serve like I was serving Jesus. I was passionate about going to religious activities. I believed in the importance of being involved in worship, but to my folly, I never ever thought that studying my heart out brought glory to Jesus. The more I read Scripture in college, the more I realized that I could put on weight for Jesus even in the environment of the classroom.

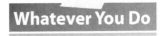

The Apostle Paul used a phrase a few times in the New Testament that really resonated with me when I was in college: "Whatever you do, do it all to the glory of God." In one location, he tells the people that even concerning what you eat, drink, or any activity in which you are involved, your purpose should be to bring about glory to God (1 Cor. 10:31). He also states that "whatever you do, in word or deed, do everything in the name of the Lord Jesus, giving thanks to God the Father through him" (Col. 3:17). My words, my thoughts, my actions, my papers, my studying, and every other area in my life should be done in the name of Jesus. If I am studying in the name of Jesus, I should study in a worthy manner.

Paul also wrote that "whatever you do, work heartily, as for the Lord and not for men, knowing that from the Lord you will receive the inheritance as your reward. You are serving the Lord Christ" (Col. 3:23-24). As I left my Greek class that day angry towards my professor, I originally wanted to do well in Greek to prove to him that I was not a slacker. Pride wanted me to stick it to him. At three in the morning, when I was writing out Greek parsing paradigms, anger towards a professor was insufficient. The desire to please your parents will not be enough to sustain you in those difficult times of study.

When I began to wrap my head around the fact that when I studied as much as I could and did my absolute best on that Greek test, God got the glory, I really started studying. I started seeing my studies as an effort to serve Christ and not impress man. Once I reached that place, not only did my attitude change but also my grades. I desired to be the absolute best I could be in the classroom.

Jesus once told a parable concerning a man who entrusted talents to his servants (Matt. 25:14-30). A talent represented about twenty years of wages for a laborer. This man gave one servant five talents, another servant two talents, and the final servant one talent. When this man returned, the first two servants had earned him more by actually doubling his investment. The man praised the two men who had been faithful stewards by exclaiming, "Well done, good and faithful servant. You have been faithful over a little; I will set you over much. Enter into the joy of your master" (Matt. 25:21).

The third servant did something very different with the money. He dug a hole and let it sit there until his master returned in order that nothing unfortunate happen to the investment. The master was not happy with him at all calling him wicked and slothful. He took away that investment from that man and gave it to the one who had actually done something with what had been entrusted to him. In a similar parable, Jesus stated, "To whom much is given, much is required" (Luke 12:48).

These statements reveal Jesus' thoughts concerning stewardship. While these words can apply to financial stewardship, it appears that Jesus was speaking to a fuller stewardship of one's own life. Applying this concept to the idea of your mind, have you ever wondered what Jesus thought about what you have done with the gifts he has given you?

He has given you a mind. Even if you do not believe that you are the sharpest person on your campus, you did make it onto a campus. You at least possess the mental capacity to enroll in college which means you have a sufficient amount of knowledge. If you are barely making it through your courses, would you call that glorifying God with your mind?

He has also given you a campus. While I am well aware that every college professor does not make the world stop during lectures due to their profound knowledge and mesmerizing teaching abilities, you are still among a small percentage in the world comprising the privileged elite to be able even to attend classes. To whom much is given, much is required. If you have been given the gift of a college education (a gift that many around this world would gladly take your place if you didn't want it), God requires of us that we be found faithful.

Instead of merely getting through college with a piece of university-stamped paper to show for your efforts, what if you saw this chance as an opportunity to invest the talents which God has invested in you? What if you decided to glorify God with your mind and make a return on his investment into your life? I have seen too many college students take the gift of an education and bury it in the ground. God is never pleased when we apathetically waste a gift from his hands. If he has given you so much, you must be mindful that he now requires something from you.

When I started teaching religion courses at a university, I was reminded at how little some students would invest into their education. I remembered what it was like to be in their position. I knew how college life was perceived to be about nonstop fun, and classes were a necessary distraction from the real college experience. Sitting at the other end of the classroom now as a teacher, I regretted so much the wasted moments and courses I experienced in college.

As students would come to class unprepared with meager attempts at scholarship, I would often think about what Jesus thought about their attempts to love him with their minds. One obviously bright student I counseled with always turned in his work late and did poorly on the tests. In a world religions course, this vibrant Christian young man was tanking quickly. When I asked him what he wanted to get out of this class, he said he wanted to learn about other religions because his intense desire was to become a missionary.

I attempted to explain that missionary organizations hire people who finish college and who finish the process well. I explained how linguistic study in a foreign country is difficult. I tried to help him see that his studies could be used as worship to Jesus, but he just never allowed that thought to register deep down in his spirit.

On the other hand, I had students in that course who wanted to be doctors, coaches, and teachers who were studying the curriculum of that course like crazy. When I read the essays on their exams, tears would literally come to my eyes because I could tell how badly they wanted to own this information. While I know that God is pleased with missionary intentions, I believe that God is equally impressed with students desiring to take a normal job in their home town but represent very well in the classroom and in the work place.

If you are at a Christian college and desiring to go into ministry, you need to do well in the classroom because you are being trained to go into the challenging vocation of taking the gospel to a broken world. I would not want a doctor operating on me who barely passed through medical exams. I do not want a minister preaching the Word of God to me who barely could make it through New Testament seminar due to lack of motivation to excel at the subject matter. If you are going into the ministry, your efforts in the classroom should be taken so seriously that you daily take in and give out what you are learning.

If your aspiration is to take the gospel to a local community or a foreign field, do not neglect this preparation time. Do not simply gain head knowledge aside from application in your classes. Serve, preach, and go while you are in college, but do not miss out on this opportunity to be prepared for the long haul of ministry. Ministry is a tough, long road, and you will need all the equipping you can receive. Paul prepared for three years before embarking upon his missionary journeys. Jesus prepared thirty years for three years of active ministry. It is interesting to note that Jesus spent ninety percent of his life training for the ten percent of his life spent actively ministering. Contrastingly, we normally spend ten percent of the time in training for the ninety percent of time we will minister before the majority of ministers retire. Find the balance of being active in ministry in the midst of studying. Don't excel at a ministry sprint when God desires you for the marathon.

If you are not a student at a Christian college, but you are a Christian on a liberal campus, you still need to represent Christ in the classroom. In Christ himself are all the "treasures of wisdom and knowledge" (Col. 2:3). Your attempts in the classroom are striving to ascertain wisdom and knowledge, and all truth is God's truth that he has bestowed upon his creation.

> As you work through your major and work towards a job, for the sake of Jesus, do not do it halfway.

If you are not planning to receive a paycheck from a Christian institution once you leave college, I do not want you to buy into the lie that you are not in the ministry. Your workplace and your classroom is a mission field, and you need to bring your gifts and passions to these environments, and be the absolute best that you possibly can be for Christ. Jesus told his disciples to "let your light shine before others, so that they may see your good works and give glory to your Father who is in heaven" (Matt. 5:16). Peter stated, "Keep your conduct among the Gentiles honorable, so that when they speak against you as evildoers, they may see your good deeds and glorify God on the day of visitation" (1 Pet. 2:12).

Do you see the similarities of these verses? As Christians, we are to be the absolute best that we can be among other believers, not so that they will praise us, but in order that they will praise Jesus. We are to excel not to build our miniature kingdoms, but to shine a light on the Kingdom of God.

History displays a stark contrast to present reality. Years ago, the greatest paintings, musical scores, and architectural pieces were almost always produced by followers of Jesus. The most talented painters painted biblical scenes because no greater image could ever fill a canvas. If a composer developed a beautiful symphony, he must put it to Scripture because no greater lyrics could possibly exist. Architectural pieces that caught the eye always drew the heart towards a mighty God.

Nowadays, Christian production has been diminished to cheesy t-shirts, mediocre films, and bad music. When a Christian artist sells his records based upon an advertisement equating his music as sounding like the music of some worldly artist, we have totally missed the concept of stewardship of the mind. We shouldn't have to compare Christians' efforts as to those who don't know Jesus; our quality of work should be greater than anything this world has to offer because we have a more magnificent subject in which to highlight, and the original Creator God lives inside of us equipping us to represent him and represent him well.

As you work through your major and work towards a job, for the sake of Jesus, do not do it halfway. Whatever you do, do it all do the glory of Jesus. It doesn't really matter what you do as long as you do it in such a way to shine a light on Jesus.

Excelling Humbly

The danger with excelling in the classroom comes through the agent of pride. Paul stated that knowledge puffs up and can make one prideful (1 Cor. 8:1). Contrastingly, Solomon stated that humility accompanies wisdom (Prov. 11:2). Mere knowledge will make you prideful, but wisdom ushers in humility. If you are allowing God to make you wise, humility will accompany you during your time in college because you know that you are merely a steward of God's gifts.

Since we know that our good works are supposed to shine for Jesus, it is wonderful to know that he has illuminated our hearts with the "knowledge of the glory of God in the face of Jesus Christ" (2 Cor. 4:6). To ensure our humility, Paul reminds us though that we have this treasure of the knowledge of him in "jars of clay, to show that the surpassing power belongs to God and not to us" (2 Cor. 4:7). Even when we excel, we excel because Jesus has equipped us to do so. Apart from him, we can do nothing (John 15:5).

The goal of excelling in the classroom is nothing less than influence. You want people to recognize that you are serious about your development. When you do well in the classroom, while you may suffer being branded as a nerd, you truly gain influence with people. The influence is not the end, but it is the means to impact your professors and classmates for Christ.

Excelling humbly does not mean that if you get a good grade in a paper, you inform the professor that God wrote that paper. If God wrote that paper, then the professor may feel inclined to give God that good grade. As you succeed in your academics, you will gain the respect and influence that a follower of Christ should receive, and you humbly receive those gifts. Unfortunately, Christians are too often labeled as using spirituality as a crutch and never forcing to think for themselves. When you love the Lord your God with all of your mind, you are defying the stereotype and earning a chance to speak into the lives of those around you. When they see your commitment and your results, you have earned the right to tell them why you want to excel.

If you gain the admiration of your college community and never turn the spotlight on Jesus, you have missed the purpose of loving God with all your mind. Excel in the classroom, but do it in such a way as to gain an opportunity to shine the light on Jesus.

It's All Greek to Me

My final exam of that first Greek course was liberating. I walked in that classroom prepared for that exam more than I had ever been prepared for anything in my life. I had depleted a stash of dry erase markers on a whiteboard in my dorm where I studied relentlessly for that class. I memorized a ton of vocabulary words. I studied in the evening, and I studied in the early hours of the morning. One morning, as I tried not to wake up my roommate, I quietly repeated Greek words and parsings from memory. He woke up to discover me sitting up in my bed with my eyes closed muttering foreign words under my breath. As I looked up, Freaky P. said, "T., when did you get the gift? Man, I didn't know that you could speak in tongues!"

I studied a lot. The more I studied, the more I understood the language in which the New Testament was written. When I placed that final exam on my professor's desk, I told him that I enjoyed that test, and that I would see him next semester.

I ended up taking five semesters of Greek. The final semester was an independent study. By the time all those classes were done, I had my own English translation of the Book of Matthew and the Book of Revelation. I am not naturally gifted in the area of academics. I struggle in languages, and I am a chronic slacker, but once I understood the necessity to love the Lord my God with all of my mind, giving weight to Jesus in the classroom was a pure joy. Will you decide to love God with *all* of your mind?

Group Questions

Chapter 11: the Classroom

Love the LORD your God will all your mind.

1. If you received a grade for your *efforts* at your school or job right now, what grade would you receive and why?

2. Why would God desire Christians to do all things for the glory of God?

3. Read Matthew 25:14-30. As God has invested passions and abilities into your life, which one of these servants would you say you have acted like and why?

4. Do you have a dream of something great you want to be involved in during your life? What is it?

5. In order to see that dream happen, how should you change your current practices to allow God's preparation in your life?

Pray that God helps you love him with all of your mind. Pray that your efforts in the classroom and in the workplace bring honor to his name.

the **Time**

Don't prioritize your schedule, schedule your priorities.

During my sophomore year, my dorm became a 24-7 social hall. Just the right motley crew of guys living in that dorm brought about an environment of hysteria with a touch of mayhem. I never recall a dull, quiet moment in that dorm. Not only did the guys living in the dorm have a great time, but also we experienced many exiles from other dorms who would just stay in our dorm all throughout the day and the night. People would sleep on our couches. Sometimes I'd find a random guy in my bathroom. My girlfriend would call my dorm room and some drifter that I didn't even know would answer, and I wouldn't even be in the room. Without exception, every hour throughout the day, something crazy was happening in our dormitory during those blessed years.

The year before that reality, my roommate and I lived in the same dorm, but it was definitely a different place. No one hung out together. Everyone would walk through the hall, go to their respective room, and lock the doors. The only time that I got to know any of the guys in my dorm was when I blew up a microwave with a volatile bag of popcorn. To aid in removing the smell of toxic popcorn, I decided to let the microwave run for a long time in a dorm closet unaware that it backed up to the ventilation system in that dorm. When every room in the dorm began to obtain that horrid smell, I got to finally meet every guy in my dorm. I just wished they had seen the humor in the whole thing.

The following year, we saw a dramatic turn around. Most people just kept their doors open all the time because you never wanted to miss out what was transpiring down the hall.   We always had four people playing on an old school Nintendo 64 Bond's Goldeneye game. Since we added couches and a great sound system to the lobby, people stayed in the lobby all the time.   Thursday nights were always the best.   For whatever reason, the long week caused us to lose our minds on Thursday nights, and we would have a little fun before going back to studying.   Depending upon the week, we might have been developing a slip and slide for the hallway, riding the no parking signs down the stairwell, or throwing footballs at my roommate's chest.

Our RA became annoyed and concerned at the amount of fun we were having in our dorm. He wanted the quiet hours to be enforced throughout the entire day, and when he saw that people congregated in our dorm, it just made him a tad agitated.   Therefore, he contacted the Dean of Students to lead a personal development seminar on time management solely for our dorm. On a Tuesday night, our entire dorm rounded up in our plush lobby to listen to a lecture on time management.

The Dean began to inform us that we had to do more in college than merely have fun. He told us that we needed to take time to study and make good grades because that is what we were there for in the first place. He also reminded us that either our parents were paying a lot of money or we were borrowing a lot of money for our education, and so we didn't need to let it go to waste. Our RA had told him that all we did was goof-off and that we had to be near failing out, and he was hoping our Dean was going to take away our fun.

The Dean asked us, "Are you guys struggling in classes? What's your GPA's?" He actually wanted us to respond, and so we did. Not every guy in our dorm could respond in this manner, but for most of the guys, they could respond that they had very good GPAs. We also had a couple of presidents of large campus organizations in our dorm.   The school's publication editor lived there. We had two of the football team's leader, and for the most part, everyone was making very good grades. The Dean looked befuddled, and stated, "Well, if you guys can accomplish this in college and do all the other stuff you are doing, have at it." Then as he began to search through our video game stash in the lobby, he asked, "Do you guys have the new football game yet? My son and I love it!"

While we laughed our heads off that night at how that seminar concluded, it actually did serve as a good reminder for the guys in my dorm. Our Dean reminded us that there is a time for studying and a time for playing. There is a time and a season for everything (Ecc. 3:1). We did know that every college student is capable of making some decisions regarding his or her time that could drastically affect his or her collegiate outcome. The guys in my dorm knew how to have a really good time. We had a blast together, and we loved college life, but we also constantly reminded each other the main reason we enrolled in college, and we did have a constant struggle in the area of time.

 Time is one of those things that you can never get back. We all have an appointed time to live, and we will not see another second of it. Everyone has a certain purpose to live for on this earth, and when that purpose is accomplished, our time is done (Acts 13:36). No magic wand will ever be able to reclaim the time you wasted yesterday. You will never be able to make up the time that you have wasted when you needed to be working on your upcoming paper. Time is slowly ticking away for each of us, and we must decide how we are going to spend what is left of the time given us.

In college, as is often the case, most students find one extreme when it comes to the area of time. Some party all of their time away and have to withdraw from classes due to excessive absences. Some students study their entire time away and never have time to enjoy God-given relationships. Some students religiously procrastinate completing their work due to the lure of keeping up with their friends on the internet and have to submit incomplete and lacking work to their professors, but a healthy balance exists when it comes to time.

Paul told the Ephesian church, "Look carefully then how you walk, not as unwise but as wise, making the best use of the time, because the days are evil" (Eph. 5:15-16). This world has seen numerous people who have walked unwisely, but it is remarkable that Paul equated wise walking or living to someone who makes the best use of time given to him. The Apostle revealed that there are plenty of ways to use our time in this life, but a most effective option of using our time always exists. Plenty of opportunities will present themselves to us on how to waste time, but we must acknowledge that God has the right and the ability to deem what is the best use. Since the danger normally lies in the extremes, let me show you the areas in which you want to stay clear.

 I love to read the Book of Proverbs because it gives you memorable statements of truth concerning how to become a wise person. If we want to live wisely, like Paul said, especially in the area of time, then it would benefit us to see what Solomon wrote in the Book of Proverbs concerning the area of time. King Solomon, one of the wisest men in the world's history, points us to legends when it comes to time management. If Solomon was going to show us how to live when it came to time, he was going to point us to one particular place: the time management skills of ants.

Most of you might be shocked to know that the Bible esteems the practices of ants when it comes to life, but for those of you who had an ant farm when you grew up, you might understand this concept better. Ants are busy. They don't slow down. They are in constant motion. They are always moving and always contributing. Solomon told us to look to them as he says, "Go to the ant, O sluggard; consider her ways and be wise...How long will you lie there, O sluggard? When will you arise from your sleep? A little sleep, a little slumber, a little folding of the hands to rest, and poverty will come upon you like a robber, and want like an armed man" (Prov. 6:6-11).

If procrastination is a frequent commodity in your life, maybe you need to look to the ants. If your social life consists of playing video games for more hours than you spend interacting with other people, maybe you need to look to the ants. If you sleep all the time and don't feel like you contribute anything to society, then perhaps you need the ants spilled into your bed to awake you. When you study the lives of ants, you notice that constant motion is characteristic of their lives, and Solomon says this routine is wise. They get stuff done! However, many college students epitomize laziness and buck against productivity.

I remember the first week of college. I remember the joy I felt after my ten o'clock class that I was able to go back to my room and do whatever I wanted. I loved the days when I would go to a nine o'clock class and then come back and get in the bed. College, while it is a busy time, is a distinct environment that can cause you to become extremely lazy and unproductive. It can cause you to become ineffective in many different areas.

The first area that laziness can affect you is the quality of your schoolwork. I am a recovering "procrastination-aholic." In high school, it drove my mom crazy that I would wait to the absolute last minute before doing my work. In college, I mastered the art of procrastination. I discovered that I worked faster under pressure and I regularly submitted papers literally hot off the press. I got the work done, but I knew it wasn't my best. I was content with the grades I received, but deep down, I knew I could do better.

I used the excuse that all the work piled up on me. I would whine to professors that they all gave us huge projects or test on the same week, but I normally knew about the work in advance. The stress that I put myself under resulted in a lack of quality in my work that was no one's fault except my own. I was the problem. My professors rarely threw curve balls at us. Their syllabi were normally consistent and accurate at projecting due dates. I was just slack.

The second area in which laziness devastated some of my college friends was that of accomplishment. By this one, I simply mean, laziness kept may of my dear fiends from ever doing anything to contribute to society. Represented on my campus, there were plenty of opportunities to join clubs or be members of service organizations. We had tons of intramural activities for those who liked to get out there and play, but laziness kept many people from fully enjoying college life.

While college keeps you busy, due to the open hours in your schedule, you actually have more available time to serve a worthy cause than any other time in your life. No matter where your college is, I promise you that there is a volunteer organization that could use some help. When you get a job, you won't be able to spend two hours on a Thursday afternoon to mentor a child after school, but in college, you could possibly make that time. You could find a soup kitchen, a church youth group, or a tutoring program where you could give back, but laziness will cause you to be selfish with your time. I am not against playing video games or instant messaging friends, but I constantly evaluate my time and wonder if I am using my time wisely.

 Another major area that laziness affected was my personal relationship with Jesus. College was the time when I knew that if I was going to grow spiritually that it was my personal, conscious decision that no one else could make for me. To grow in my knowledge of God, I needed to know more about him by reading the Bible more. I never realized that staying up all night could possibly affect that relationship. Once you pull your first all-nighter, you know you have officially reached full-fledged college status. For some reason, pulling an all-nighter in college is a nostalgic event that cements your standing as legit. What I never realized was that the stress of having to cram for a test could hinder my walk with Christ. Instead of daily keeping up on my class work, I would have to pull an all-nighter to catch up, and then the next morning I wouldn't have energy to get up and spend time with Jesus, and somehow throughout the hysteria of my dorm life, it seemed impossible to get alone.

I desired to change, but I was like that man of whom Solomon spoke. How long would I sleep? Would I ever get up? I hit the snooze button like it was my job. One day, I simply got fed up with my spiritual condition, and I wanted more. So I placed my alarm clock further away from my bed so I couldn't easily turn it off. When I woke in the morning to the horrid sound of my alarm clock, I had to strain to reach the snooze button which caused me to get going in the morning.

I know that everyone needs a different amount of hours of sleep everyday. My wife needed at least eight hours of sleep every night in college or else she couldn't function the next day. She would be amazed at how little sleep I needed. She was also appalled at the fact that she would call me after studying and getting ready to go to bed, and the guys in my room were working on a math equation concerning how far our water balloon launcher could travel. Everyone needs a different amount of sleep so that you can function in class and in life, but you can also oversleep. College students who sleep late hours into the day and take frequent naps need to evaluate if they need all that sleep or has laziness subtly taken hold in your life?

 The other extreme in the area of time is college students who are simply way too busy. When I worked with the leadership of certain campus organizations, I would always remind people that in the first two weeks, freshmen will set the course for how they are going to live for their tenure in college. In those first two weeks, they will find a core of friends and a set of clubs or organizations to which they belong. Due to that fact, our crew would always be overly intentional about reaching out to these students the first two weeks, and every other club had the same idea which led many freshmen to attend about seventy-two interest meetings their first month in college. While many people will never return to some organizations after their first visit, some college students will get involved in a few organizations, and most of these organizations demand a significant portion of your precious time.

In addition to the class load that one is carrying, a college student will decide to be an overachiever in this area and can easily get burned out. In my first few years as a college minister, I was amazed at how sporadic some students' attendance would be to our college Bible studies. It wasn't that they didn't want to come. They had a good experience, and they liked the people. They just couldn't commit because the organizations that they were a part of demanded so much time from them. A group of girls in a sorority wanted to come to church on Sunday nights, but if they missed the meeting, their sorority sisters would make them pay a fine for missing. When it was Rush Week, we should have just canceled our activities. Sports practice would keep many from being active in anything outside of their practice.

It is very easy to end your college years and be able to characterize them as frantic and rushed. One of the greatest words I ever used was one of the hardest ones to speak, but I had to discipline myself to tell people "no." I am a people-pleaser at heart. I hate when people are disappointed in me. I strive to work hard so that others will notice. Genuinely, I don't want to let anyone down.

Instead of telling someone you honestly can't attend an event or help out with an organization, you might be the type of person who would rather stress yourself out than feel as though someone is mad at you. I came to realize in college that there were plenty of *good* things on which I could spend my time or there were a few *great* things on which I could spend my time.

We throw the phrase, "doing God's will" around a lot in Christian circles (I devoted all of chapter fifteen to it). If you honestly believe that God truly put you on this earth for a specific purpose and you have a limited time upon this world to trod, then you don't have time to fill your schedule up with anything other than God's will. Have you ever thought that good things that you do based upon good intentions could actually keep you from God's will – the best things on which you can spend your time? If you are worried about disappointing someone, let me go ahead and relieve you – it is impossible to please everyone. I work in a church – I know this firsthand! If you can't please everyone with how you spend your time, you have to prioritize whom you want to please. The Apostle Paul made up his mind when he wrote, "For am I now seeking the favor of men or of God? Or am I still striving to please men? If I were still trying to please men, I would not be a bond-servant of Christ" (Gal. 1:10).

> If you honestly believe that God truly put you on this earth for a specific purpose...you don't have time to fill your schedule up with anything other than God's will.

Busy Spirituality

While you should seek to please God with your time, I know some students who have become confused on what it means to please God versus simply being religious. Some students in our town couldn't regularly commit to belong to a small group because they attended about five different Bible studies a week. I knew of some students who went to church on Sunday and some weeks would visit four to five campus Christian organizations. While they may seem spiritual to some, it appeared dangerous to me because they visited a whole lot of things, but they could never commit to one thing well. In fact, I realized that I was trying to minister to a college campus that contained students who were getting plenty of religious information, but they were not taking the time to do anything with that information. They had plenty of information, but they were lacking in the application department all because they were way too busy to do anything with what they were learning. A bond-servant of Christ puts into practice what he learns and does not simply attend religious events.

Mary and Martha were sisters who followed Jesus. On a day when Jesus visited them at their house, Martha was frantically busy trying to do so much for Jesus. Contrastingly, Mary was sitting at the feet of Jesus hanging on every word he spoke. While Jesus was teaching, Martha actually interrupted him to tattle tell on her sister, Mary. She was so upset that she was actively busy for the Lord, and all her sister was doing was being with the Lord. Jesus told Martha that she was "anxious and troubled about many things, but one thing is necessary. Mary has chosen the good portion, which will not be taken away from her" (Luke 10:41-42). It is quite possible that college students can be so busy for Jesus but miss Jesus in the process. You can attend tons of Bible studies. You might have an accountability partner. You can go to a church frequently. You can be a very religious person, but you could completely miss Christ in the whole process.

Busyness cannot foster intimacy. You have to learn how to slow down. You have to choose to be busy with a few things and not be overloaded to the point that you are no good to any of the things to which you commit yourself. Don't let religion trick you. Nothing can substitute a growing relationship with Jesus – even religious busyness. Currently, you are as close to Jesus as you have chosen to be.

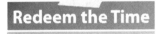

The Puritans didn't speak of spending time. They spoke of redeeming the time. Just like when Paul told the Ephesians to make the most of their time, the Puritans saw each actual second as a gift that must be spent carefully. When it comes to time, balance is key. Don't work so much that you don't have time to play, but don't play so much that you don't have time to work. You only have four years in college, but some of you realistically might have more. Regardless, the time is limited and you can never get these days back. Choose wisely. If I had a chance to do college over again, I would have redeemed my time differently.

First, I would ensure that I made time for the one thing for which I am living – Jesus. Since Jesus is the most forgiving person in your life, you will oftentimes abuse his charitable love and put him off when rivaled by any other relationship. You understand that your friends, the person you are dating, your family, or your professors are not as forgiving as he, and so we regularly put him off. The times in my life when I made him a time priority, I did disappoint some people, but I also made better use of my time throughout the day because I did the most important thing first.

Second, don't prioritize your schedule, learn to schedule your priorities. Wipe the slate clean. What is the most important things you can be a part of in your life right now? Then ruthlessly get rid off filler stuff until you can do those things. Don't waste your life. Figure out how you can give back and do whatever it takes to enable yourself to serve your King on this earth.

Third, pick one or two Christian groups to join. I did not say go to a Christian group; I want you to join it. Live with those people. Serve with those people. Cry and laugh with those people. If you are busy going to too many events, you will never belong to any group. The first group should be a local church (see chapter seven) because every campus organization will only be available when you are on campus. When you graduate, you need something to belong to during the transition. Find a church and/or a group that does two things: 1) challenges you, and 2) gives you a place to serve. If that organization can truly help you grow in Christlikeness and allow you to serve, you have found a place to belong.

Fourth, evaluate your schedule. One week, literally record everything you did on a weekly calendar. See how much time you wasted or rushed through the day. Could you have planned better for projects that were coming up? Did you take adequate time to enjoy God-given relationships? In the last week, did you worship, work, and play?

Finally, start looking for ways to eliminate time-wasters. I am not telling you not to play video games or watch chick flicks. I am encouraging you to use those times wisely as well as remove any time-wasters that could keep you from doing God's will. I let things pile up on me, but recently, I have started developing some rules so that I can redeem the time.

- Only handle a piece of paper once. If I'm going to open it, I'm either going to file it or trash it.
- Only handle an email once. If I have time to read it, I had better make time to respond to it. If I don't, I will have read an email that gets buried, and I won't respond to it till weeks later.
- Only handle a voicemail once. If I'm going to listen to it, I had better have time to respond to it. If the person who left a message is going to take a long time, I have to intentionally leave time for it.
- Play and play well, but only after the work is done. I have worked to restore the Sabbath in my life. I am working like crazy for six days, and then having the time of my life on the seventh day. What I have found is that I enjoy the six days a whole lot more now.
- Don't neglect the present reality. I often will get distracted by something way off in the future while procrastinating what has to be done that day. Choose your tasks wisely.
- Turn off distractions. Even while I am writing these words, my phone is ringing and my email reminder is popping up telling me someone else needs my attention, but right now, you, the reader, are more important to me, and I must shut those things off to concentrate (OK, that's better now).
- Always prioritize the important over the trivial. Find out what is the best way to use this day, and live it up.

After all, we've only got today once, and then it's gone. We had better spend this time wisely.

Group Questions

Chapter 12: the Time

Don't prioritize your schedule, schedule your priorities.

1. Would you consider yourself a person who studies constantly or procrastinates regularly? What is dangerous about your condition?

2. Read 2 Thessalonians 3:6-12. What kind of people does Paul warn us about becoming?

3. What are the important things for which you cannot find enough time?

4. What are the trivial things in your life that are draining your time?

5. What practical ways can you think of to begin to redeem the time in your own life?

Pray that you begin to use your time to glorify God. Pray that you fill up the seconds alloted to you in a way that pleases the one who gave them to you.

the **Family**

My family cannot change if I stay the same.

The first semester our church started a college worship service, we experienced God do some incredible things in our midst. As we neared the final service of the Fall semester, I wanted to teach on something that would prove to be very relevant over Christmas Break. Since exams were nearly over, bags were semi-packed, I wanted to prepare these college students for the inevitable spiritual conflict they would be facing within a matter of a few days: the return home.

All college students would face this dynamic. Freshmen would experience this tension in a profound way. I told them the scenario would look similar to what other students had experienced. A freshman named Sarah returns home after exams. After sleeping straight for about forty-eight hours to make up for the lack of sleep during exams, Sarah emerges from her comatose snooze. She gets a text from her high school friends that everyone is hanging out tonight. Sarah goes out with them, has a blast, and returns at the normal hour that she has returned from hanging out with her friends the last few months while she was away at school. On this fateful night, she encounters parents who are unreasonably concerned with her late night arrival. Sarah is confused because she is just continuing doing what she has done when she has been out from under their roof. Only one problem: she is residing under their roof for a month.

The scenario may look different for you. Even if that quirky scenario doesn't happen to you, make no mistake, quirky parents or guardians are unavoidable. The more independent you become, the more likely you are to face the tension associated with leaving the nest. The nearer you draw to graduation, the more you will face the conflict of finding resolution with the person who raised you.

One of my favorite movies when I was a child was the Christmas classic, *Home Alone*. When I was in elementary school, I got to watch Macaulay Culkin live out every child's fantasy on the big screen: no parents, no siblings, freedom without end, and making your home into a real war zone. The desire to be a mischievous hero marked every little boy my age.

If you remember the plot line, Culkin's character, "Kevin," had a pretty awful family. He had a brother Buzz who wanted to feed him to his tarantula. He had to bunk with his cousin Fuller who was prone to bed-wetting and was downing some serious Pepsi. Worst of all, his cheapskate Uncle Frank was known for spouting off towards Kevin one of the most memorable movie lines of all time: "Look what you did, you little jerk!"

Let's face it: Kevin did not have the best family in the world, so when they dramatically disappeared one morning before Christmas, Kevin thought he had been raptured into parent-less bliss. His wish had become true. His annoying family had been whisked away from his home.

However, Kevin wasn't the best family member in the whole world either. In fact, Kevin had a pretty big mouth and a very selfish attitude for someone so small in stature. While his family was quite annoying, he fit in with them quite well.

The Hardest Place to Live for Christ

For many college students, the hardest place to be a Christian is when they are around their family. Since this group has seen you at your worst, they have an uncanny knack at being able to provoke you to anger faster than anyone else. You have an ability to spot their faults from a mile away. Tempers flare, words fly, and an awful lot of regret is unfortunately birthed in someone's very own home.

Even if your home isn't as blatantly dysfunctional as Kevin's, your family has its issues. They probably majored in issues. I realized one day that everyone seems to have the "family crazy" somewhere in their family tree (which made me wonder, if everyone has a "family crazy," I must be the "family crazy" to someone else). It is unavoidable that you will experience some type of family drama. With your growing independence, you will start to experience a whole other level of issues as you begin to enter into adulthood cutting the ties in various ways from your family.

While it is easy to point out your family's issues, can you acknowledge your own? In reality, you will not be able to change your family members. The nature of your relationship with your parents and siblings puts them at an intense defensive level. No matter if you are right, it is simply difficult for your family members to take criticism from you. If you want to change them, you are going to have to attempt it from another angle.

If you want to change your family, you must start with yourself. Your family cannot change if you stay the same. If you anticipate a day when your family puts the fun back in functional, comes to their logical senses, and starts bending to your every desire, you can keep on waiting. If you feel a burden for your family to change, you must start the change within yourself. Before you scrutinize their miniscule faults, you must learn to remove the obvious log from your own eye (Matt. 7:5).

Honor Thy Parents

My attempt at making this a hip manual for college students just flew out the window. The very fact that I am discussing honoring one's father and mother just plummeted me to geezer status. I realize that and gladly accept that connotation. Even though you are nearing independent status, God still commands all children to honor their parents (or guardians) regardless of age or maturity.

In the Ten Commandments, God gave four vertical commands (how you relate to God) and six horizontal commands (how you relate to others). The first horizontal command is to honor your father and mother

(Ex. 20:12). Before do not kill, do not steal, or do not commit adultery, God commanded his followers to honor their parents. God must intend this commandment to be foundational to the other commands. It's interesting to note that God actually says that if someone honors his father and mother, his days will be long (Ex. 20:12).

Mere obedience to this command provides a promise of a quality life. When Moses repeated this command later in Israel's history, he included the phrase, "that your days may be long, and that it may go well with you in the land that the LORD your God is giving you" (Deut. 5:16). While one application of this command could be found in God's provision for his people in the land they were entering, God also revealed a deeper spiritual blessing that one's quality of life would be graced with God's great favor upon obedience of this command.

As Paul neared the conclusion of his letter to the Ephesians, he included instructions concerning the family. His first instructions in chapter six were for children to obey their parents (Eph 6:1). The phrase "in the Lord" is not to be understood as obeying Christian parents only, but children were expected to obey their parents regardless of the parents' spiritual standing. Paul mandated Christian children to obey their parents even if the parents were non-Christians as long as that obedience did not compete with their obedience to the Lord. For children without ideal Christian parents, honor for the individual parent may be difficult at times, but Christian children must muster honor for at least the office of parent at all times.

Paul's command to obey parents in the Lord adds a deeper spiritual implication to the command. Children must understand that when they obey their parents, they are subsequently obeying the Lord. In an ideal Christian home, parents are simply asking children to give them respect in response to the parents' own submission to Christ. Paul views this obedience so significantly that he groups disobedience to parents in a list of godless sins next to murder, greed, and other unrighteous acts (Rom 1:28-32). One of Paul's signs that the end of time is nearing is the presence of disobedient children (2 Tim 3:2). God viewed obedience to parents as so important that he imposed the death penalty on disobedient children (Lev 20:9; Deut 21:18-21). God views a disobedient child as a disgrace (Prov 19:26). In the Book of Proverbs, children are also warned concerning the danger of cursing their parents (Prov 20:20).

Paul gives no indication that problems existed in the Ephesian church concerning family relationships, but he obviously sees the need to regard family instruction as an appropriate teaching regardless of circumstances. Unfortunately for many Christians, the home is often the most difficult environment to live with the attitude of Christ (Phil 2:3-5), but Paul held this environment to be one of the most critical in which to show mutual honor. Not only does Paul instruct children to obey their parents in the Lord, but he also tells this church that obedience is simply the just act for children according to God's plan for the family.

While the term "children" could refer to adult children, Paul probably intended his message for younger children who were still impressionable and prime for spiritual molding. Paul might have intended his message for children at least in teenage years who were not old enough to live on their own but still young enough to receive discipline and instruction. Even though this commandment is meant more practically towards younger children, Jesus confronted older Pharisees for abandoning this commandment and dishonoring their parents in order to follow the traditions of men (Mark 7:9-13). As young children grow into adults, the specifics of obedience will change, but the parent's divine right of honor should never change.

While the command for children to obey their parents originated at the giving of the Ten Commandments, the New Testament includes this command five times other than this passage (Matt 15:4; 19:19; Mark 7:10; 10:19; Luke 18:20). God's original command (Exod 20:12; Deut 5:16) instructed children to obey in order to flourish in the land. Paul, speaking to Jews and Gentiles estranged from the idea of inheriting land that the original hearers anticipated, changes the ending from "live long in the land" to "live long on the earth" (Eph 6:3). This subtle shift indicates that his audience is not anticipating prospering in a certain geographical location, but they do desire for their lives to prosper in general. Paul's intention through this change was to indicate that obedience to parents provides needed structure in the lives of children.

If for no other reason, you need to honor your parents because God said so. Honestly, you shouldn't need another reason. If you do require another viable reason, you must also realize that honoring your parents brings a smile to God's face. Your submission to your parents pleases God himself (Col. 3:20). Since God created order, he has set up the institution of the home with an intended structure for mutual benefit. In an ideal home, loving parents will lead through instruction and example what it means to live for Christ. In that ideal home, children will graciously and easily submit to their leadership because it is most natural.

When college students have rebelled against this concept, I have heard rebuttals centering on Jesus' example. Jesus did say that his family was first and foremost spiritual in nature rather than based upon flesh and blood families (Matt. 12:46-50). While his stinging comment leads some to dishonor one's parents, you must be careful how you apply this concept. Jesus was simply stating that obedience to God would sometimes cause you to be ostracized from your family. Jesus never stopped honoring his family. When his mother asked him to help the catering company at a wedding, Jesus graciously did what his mother asked even if it wasn't his desired timing of performing a miracle (John 2:3-5). Upon the cross, carrying the weight of mankind's sin upon his shoulders, Jesus still mustered the strength to ensure that the Apostle John would care for his mother when he was gone (John 19:26-27).

4 Parent/Child Relationships

As I see it, you and your parents probably belong in one of four specific categories. While the family dynamics are sure to be different in every scenario, your family probably fits neatly into one of the following distinctions:

Great Parent and Great Child. This category is unfortunately the minority. This family is characterized by a great parent(s) or guardian(s) who loves God. The authorities in this house love Jesus and try to run the home in a manner that is obedient to the prescribed biblical guidelines. While the parent is not perfect, this parent is striving to live in a manner worthy of Christ's calling (Eph. 4:1).

In addition to a great parent, this home is characterized by a great child - you. Even while your life is full of constant missteps, you are trying to make your one ambition pleasing to Jesus too. Just like your parents, you are openly allowing Christ to investigate every area of your life to see if there is anything unpleasing to him (Ps. 139:23-24).

If this scenario describes your family, your logical next step is gratitude. I pray that you fathom the unparalleled privilege that you have and you praise God for his favor on a regular basis. Your family characterized by God's presence is a stark minority in our world today, and you do not need to let a day go by without sincerely praising Jesus for the gift of your family (Ps. 50:23).

Great Parent and Sorry Child. If your family is in this category, you will have a hard time spotting it. In fact, you probably won't openly admit it. So here's a test to see if this is your family: if you complain about petty things that your parents impose on you that impede your freedom minutely, you are probably in this category. I know so many students who begrudge the fact that they have good parents who are following Jesus, but they have the audacity to establish boundaries and rules for their home. Due to early curfews, limited spending, or some other non-essential area, a student devalues his or her parents by claiming they are out of touch with the times. This exaggerated reaction does everything but honor them; this attitude actually dishonors them.

If you have great parents and you are proving to be a sorry child, you don't want to admit it. Your tendency is to claim that your parents are unreasonable and you are a responsible adult deserving of more respect. How responsible are you? If your parents still provide your health insurance, pay for school fees, and possess the title to the car you drive, do you really want to follow your argument to its logical conclusion? Even if you are fiscally responsible for the majority of your bills, your parents still rightfully deserve your willful honor. If you are still mooching off of your parents, you need to change your attitude to reflect thankfulness for those who have nurtured you so.

If this scenario describes your family, your logical next step is repentance. You need to ask God and your parents for forgiveness for such a selfish disposition. If your greatest complaint concerning your parents centers upon a menial element in your life (even if it seems big to you), you need to reevaluate your priorities. One of the greatest blessings you could have is for God to introduce you to some students who don't have parents as loving and godly as yours to give you a reality check. If you saw the state of most homes, you would bewail your selfish attitude and your focus upon non-essentials. If you have been a sorry child, you need to apologize to your parents and begin to pray that you one day become a fraction of the parent they are to you.

Sorry Parent and Great Child. If your family fits neatly into this dynamic, you are a part of a growing population of young adults in our culture. If you have a parent or parents who do not love God and haven't served as the greatest role model in your life, you know the pain associated with desiring more out of your home. The amount of adults who have failed morally grow by the year. The divorce rate is 50% inside and outside of the church. Many parents are not living up to their God-given responsibility. Some fathers try to climb the corporate ladder so aggressively they miss their children growing up. Some mothers are decisively bent upon living their lives through their children that they miss their children's blessed individuality. Many parents have fallen in the areas of sexual immorality, greed, pride, and emotional instability. No matter what the symptom is, the reality is that many parents are not treasuring a relationship with God, and the status of their lives just simply proves it (Isa. 48:18).

In this scenario, you would have to be a child attempting to live for Jesus. While you are nowhere near perfect, your heart does desire to follow Jesus. The more you read the words of Scripture, the more your heart breaks for your parents. You know that their lives would move towards stability if they would simply surrender to Christ, but you struggle with how and if you should tell them that. You feel tension in your home due to your spiritual growth. The more you grow, the more you want to change, and oftentimes, you find resistance from your very own parents. They don't understand that your quest for purity is why you want to get married earlier than the national average. They struggle with comprehending your desire to spend a summer serving an unknown people group in an unreached area when you could be working in an internship to propel your career after college. Your growth is not inspirational to them but can actually serve as an annoyance.

If this scenario is similar to your home setting, your critical next step is perseverance. As long as obedience to your parents does not conflict with your obedience to Christ (which is rarely the case), you are to continue to honor them. Even if honor for the person is difficult, honor for the office of parent is a biblical mandate. I promise you that you will not change your parents by preaching them sermons at such a young age on how you have figured out everything in life in which they are failing. Arrogance on your part will not lead to repentance on their part. You need to lovingly submit to your parents even if they aren't close with the Lord. Just like Paul stated in Ephesians 6, your obedience to your parents serves as an indication of your obedience to your God. Your gracious respect can go a long way in their lives. Your respect doesn't condone their actions or approves of their disobedience, but it can serve as a glaring sign for your parents that something is changing inside of you. They are aware that you disagree with their lifestyle, but your obedience to Christ proves to them that you are committing entirely to the obedience of Christ.

Sorry Parent and Sorry Child. This last scenario is pretty self-explanatory. Your parent doesn't desire to obey Christ and neither do you. Maybe you are associated with God (you call on him when in need), but you really don't nurture your relationship with God. All you have seen in your parents is a casual acquaintance with Jesus and that is all you have ever had yourself due to their example.

If you have sorry parents who are not following God, may I ask why you would want to continue behind them in their spiritual legacy? If they are not peaceful, respectable, reliable, or compassionate, do you just merely hope you won't end up like them? In reality, your parents, no matter how unintentional they were in your maturation, have left an incredible impact on how you will function as an adult and how you will relate to your own spouse and children one day. If this is your case, you simply need to change.

Casey was a college student with a tragic story. Her family drama was more chaotic than the juiciest of talk shows. Her mother was not a nurturing mother; her estranged father was a drifter and a drunk, and the rest of her family was known by their instability. While Casey started out college desiring an alternative ending to her story, she slowly started to drift away from God's ideal. She began to drink her anxiety away completely oblivious that she was following in her father's footsteps which she had cursed for so many years. Her isolation from the rest of her family was turning into the same type of behavior characteristic of family members of whom she had complained. Before she knew it, her disgust for her family was leading her to be blind to her own toxic spiritual issues.

There comes a time in everyone's life when you have to decide if you want to lay down the crutches or not. I had a friend that was a bit of a hypochondriac. If he slightly twisted his ankle, he would put on ace bandages, strut on a limp, and not be caught without his trusty crutches. While he did hurt his leg at one time, he continually ran back to his crutches for attention and sympathy from others when his healing had been complete for a long time.

> No amount of instability could compete with the stability he brought into your heart when you surrendered to him.

Spiritually speaking, some of you need to lay aside your crutches. The pain you experienced from your parents is real. The damage that they caused is a genuine reality, but if you truly know the actual and total healing present in a relationship with Jesus, you will not walk around on crutches the rest of your life. You will not allow your mother's critical spirit to fester into your other relationships. You will not repeat your father's uncommitted devotion to Christ. You will bring the pitiful spiritual legacy of your family to a screeching halt once you decide that what Christ did for you at the cross outweighs what your parents did or didn't do in the home.

Even if your earthly father was a worthless example to you, you have a Heavenly Father that delivered hope into your hopeless home. He was able to bring healing to your brokenness. No amount of instability could compete with the stability that he brought into your heart when you surrendered to him. You must become contented as you realize that no amount of parental deficiencies can compare to the sufficiency of your heavenly Father. While your pain is real and your disappointment true, it is time to put down your crutches and walk in the newness of what Christ has to offer you. Defy your parent's spiritual legacy and start a new one that can turn the course of generations behind you (Ex. 20:6). The best way to change your parents is to change yourself.

 While another dynamic is your sibling relationships, I can easily answer that one for you: "As far as it depends on you, live at peace with all men" (Rom. 12:18). This practical command works for sibling rivalries and estranged parents. No matter what your family dynamic is, you need to let the grace of Jesus infect you to display grace to your family members. That verse doesn't state that every attempt will be successful. You are not responsible for how they respond, but you are responsible for how you react. Your job in your family is to be a grace-giver.

Depending upon your family situation, the direct application for you varies. You either need to thank God, repent, persevere, or change. You need to start investing in your family and no longer wait for their move. Your family cannot and will not change if you stay the same. You need to begin to change not only for your current family's sake, but also for the sake of the generations behind you.

A buddy of mine, Ben, and I were groomsmen in a friend's wedding when we were in college. At the rehearsal dinner, both sets of parents got up and told of how they had prayed for their child's spouse from the day their child was born. This dinner was not the roasting that you often see. These families led in a worship service. I will never forget Ben looking at me with tears in his eyes and stating he wished that he could have this type of service for his rehearsal dinner. With the state of his family, we both knew that was unrealistic. In hope, I told him, "You may not be able to enjoy this for your wedding, but that doesn't have to be your kids' story."

No matter what your situation is, it doesn't have to stay that way. If you want your family to glorify God, be the catalyst among them rather than the holy roller judging them. Your family cannot change if you stay the same.

Group Questions

Chapter 13: the Family

My family cannot change if I stay the same.

1. Why is it difficult to live for Christ around your family?

2. Which parent/child relationship describes your situation best?

3. Read Colossians 3:12-17. Which of these descriptive phrases should you begin to utilize with your family right now?

4. In order to change your family, what area do you personally need to change first?

5. In thinking about your own family you may start one day, what principles do you want to lead your family to adhere?

Pray that your family would change for the glory of God. Pray that the change begins in you.

the **World**

*The Great Commission is not a suggestion to be considered
but a commandment to be obeyed.*

It wasn't that I had anything against missions; I just had never really seen a need for me personally to go.   Since I had become a Christian, I understood the need for Jesus' followers to spread his gospel all over the world, but I never saw that act as a priority for my personal life. Overseas missions was for that group of people who were so spiritual they needed to live among some unknown tribe because they could no longer function normally in American society.

The summer after my freshman year, I was accepted into a training program called The Laborer's Institute, a ministry of Kingdom Building Ministries. Consisting of three months, the program led college students through one month of intense discipleship training, one month of overseas missions, and one month of work in youth camps around the United States. Since the overseas missions part was sandwiched in the two months in which I was truly interested, I merely saw my upcoming time overseas as an item to mark off of a super-spiritual checklist. Expecting to experience some pretty incredible things, I never really saw this experience as changing literally everything in my life, but it did.

I'll never forget the night when my world got a little bit bigger. During a college worship service in Kokobujni Baptist Church in Tokyo, Japan, I experienced a foretaste of heaven. As our team worshiped to a song in English, our Japanese brothers and sisters joined in with their beautiful language, and I heard the melodies of heaven. Two languages worshiping one God ushered in what John reported in the Book of Revelation: "After this I looked and there before me was a great multitude that no one could count, from every nation, tribe, people and language, standing before the throne and in front of the Lamb" (Rev. 7:9).

For the first time, I saw God outside of my American context. I saw Jesus as not merely the Savior of those in the Bible Belt, but I saw him as the Lamb of God who takes away the sins of the entire world (John 1:29). I saw his Kingdom advancing all over the world, and all of a sudden, my perception of Jesus got exceedingly larger. He didn't become more powerful, but I perceived him as more powerful. My month overseas earned me more than funny stories about cultural customs or interesting pictures of unique food; I learned the value of the Great Commission. Without a doubt, one of the greatest blessings God ever gave me to grow me up spiritually in college was getting out of the United States and seeing him work all over the world.

The Great Suggestion

The Great Commission is not a suggestion to be considered but a command to be obeyed. Before Jesus ascended into heaven, he told his disciples that all authority in heaven and on earth had been given to him. He then told them, "Go therefore and make disciples of all nations, baptizing them in the name of the Father and of the Son and of the Holy Spirit, teaching them to observe all that I have commanded you. And behold, I am with you always, to the end of the age" (Matt. 28:18-20).

Jesus was not offering a suggestion for his followers to consider, he was giving them the framework from how they were now supposed to live their lives. His wording was very intentional. Jesus desired for his followers to make disciples, not merely converts. Our goal is not to leave converts directionless after they become saved. We are not merely collecting numbers of conversions in order to impress other people. Our goal is to make full-fledged disciples of every single nation in the world. We are to baptize them among other believers so they have an entourage to help them grow spiritually. As Jesus concluded, he offered the greatest encouragement ever that he personally would be with us as we go.

Unfortunately, the majority of Christians view Jesus' missionary call as nothing more than a suggestion for the religious elite, but his call is for all those who call on his name. We know in order to make him known. I hope that you go on an overseas mission trip before you graduate. An experience like that cannot return you the same. While the excuses I used concerning why I shouldn't have to go overseas may differ than your personal ones, I have found that all of the top ten excuses fall into one of the following categories: comfort, circumstances, or commitment.

 Even if you are someone who claims to "rough it," most people are apprehensive about packing up and going to some foreign place in which they can't even spell the name of the country. Fear of rough living conditions, strange food, and uncomfortable social customs keep people from taking the leap out of a comfort zone onto the mission field. One thing that I have found in my time overseas is that the most comfortable place is to be in the center of God's will. If God has called you to a place, no uncomfortable conditions can compare to the peace that floods your heart when you are obedient to his call.

10. *"I couldn't survive in rough conditions."* If you are worried that you could not survive in rough conditions, there is a possibility that you have become a little too pampered. If the comfort associated with physical luxuries can keep you away from the lost of the world, then maybe removing yourself from those elements is exactly what you need. Paul described godliness as extremely beneficial when accompanied by contentment. Since we brought nothing into this world, he reminds that we will not leave with anything either, and if we have simple food and covering, we should feel nothing less than contentment (1 Tim. 6:6-8). Maybe a little detachment from your luxuries could serve as a healthy reminder that this world is not our home.

9. *"I fear for my safety."* The more that our world becomes informed through worldwide media, it is easy to become fearful of unsafe conditions. Fear of disease, war, or travel keep many people from leaving the shores of the United States. If you haven't noticed, the United States is not the most secure place in the world either. Calamities happen in our own country as much as other countries. If you truly believe that greater is he who is in you than he who is in the world (1 John 4:4), then you cannot rightfully fear the troubles of this world. As Jesus spoke to the need of taking the gospel to all nations, he promised that those who found themselves in unsafe conditions should not be anxious, for the Holy Spirit would speak through them and guide them (Mark 13:10-11). The safest place in the world is always where God is leading you.

8. *"I couldn't eat the food."* This excuse has been a major prayer request for college students that I have taken on the field. Picky eaters really deliberate whether or not they can withstand certain meals. A little digestive problems never slow down a committed missionary. While you do have to adjust to food and customs with which you may not be comfortable, you have to choose the gospel over comfort. Paul said he knew what it felt like to eat your fill and to be in want, but he had learned to do all things since Christ gave him strength (Phil. 4:12-13).

7. *"I would miss my family and friends."* Jesus shocked a group of listeners one day when he stated, "If anyone comes to me and does not hate his father and mother, his wife and children, his brothers and sisters, yes, even his own life, he cannot be my disciple" (Luke 14:26). Jesus used this statement as an exaggeration to show the level of our commitment to him should be so great compared to our commitment to others that the chasm between the two would appear as if we hated our family. Our call is first to follow our God; he gives us those relationships as a blessing, but they were never intended to usurp his position in our lives. You will have moments of missing those special people in your life, but I promise you that if you are obedient to God's call, you will be a better person for them once you return.

 **Circumstances**

While many comfort excuses exist, differing circumstances often serve as deterrents from going on a mission trip as well. These types of excuses either look at personal inadequacies or overwhelming odds as an indication of God's leading that they are not called to go. As you read the Bible, you must see that God often used extenuating circumstances to reveal his power in people's weaknesses (2 Cor. 12:9-10). Below is a list of popular excuses that fall in the circumstances category.

6. *"I do not know enough about the Bible."* If you wait until you have a firm grasp on the totality of God's Word, you will never make it to the nations. The greatest biblical scholar in the world still has so much to learn about the riches of the Bible. Even if someone understood all there was to know about the Bible, the application of its message is more important than the information presented. Jesus once told his disciples, "My food is to do the will of him who sent me and to finish his work" (John 4:34). Getting spiritually "fed" is not knowing information, it is applying the information you know, and if you know that God's Word says to go, the most important thing is to be found obedient not to understand some deeper, hidden meaning.

5. *"I do not have the time."* When college students discern whether or not they should go on a short term trip over a summer, many reply that they simply do not have enough time. I have found that we always make time for the things that are important to us. We are told to make the most of our time because the days are full of evil distractions (Eph. 5:15-16). If our entire being is wrapped up in being God's ambassadors (2 Cor. 5:20), then we will not fill our schedule up with trivial matters if we have not committed time to the greatest need in the world: to make Jesus' name known to the nations.

4. *"I don't have enough money to go."* Plane tickets are not getting cheaper by the year. The cost of traveling to another country, even if the living conditions are not great, is expensive. If Jesus calls you, he can send you. No travel expenses causes Jesus to stay up at night unable to rest. Paul, when speaking to a church concerning his financial means for ministry, stated, "My God will meet all your needs according to his glorious riches in Christ Jesus" (Phil. 4:19). God claims to have all the riches in the world (Ps. 50:10); he is not in need or anxious concerning how to fund his ambassadors relentlessly pursuing the nations. If you step out in faith to go overseas, you will be amazed at how God stretches your faith to see how he provides. His provision will come from the most unlikely places sometimes. His provision may also come from your personal sacrifice. I went to Asia two summers when I was in college.

One trip was completely paid for by givers in my church, and another trip was completely paid for by my summer job. I praise God for those who gave the first time, but I offered God praise by desiring my hard earned money to give some people without access to the gospel a chance at hearing the name of Jesus. If you truly want to go, you will find a way to go.

3. *"God couldn't use me because of my past."* Many people, overwhelmed with regrets concerning past mistakes, feel immobile due to an incorrect belief that God only uses perfect people. If your life was spotless, you wouldn't need the gospel yourself let alone have a reason to give it to someone else. God is the only one able to use our past, including our mistakes, for a greater good (Rom. 8:28). In your frailties and insufficiencies, God is able to shine all the brighter. As imperfect people reaching out to imperfect people, Jesus' gospel stands out against all other religions. We could not reach God due to good works; Jesus reached out to us. A reliance upon our personal worthiness is a negation of the gospel. Praise God that he saved you from your past. If he can save you, then he can save others!

2. *"I am not called to do missions."* I often wonder about people's definition of God's calling when it comes to missions. I do not believe that every person is called to spend their entire lives on the foreign field. I *do* believe that every Christian's life is supposed to be focused upon reaching those that do not know Jesus. We go to our campuses, our workplaces, and the nations. Make no mistake about it, as a Christian, you are called to be a missionary. I can't say what field for which you are called, but I do know Jesus expects you to go. It is interesting that we ask God to repeat his assignment. Why do we make God repeat that which he has already commanded? Paul wrote that Jesus has committed to us the ministry of reconciliation (2 Cor. 5:19). No matter the field, we are missionaries by our association with Christ. If you are called to be a missionary in America to your workplace, praise God, but I also dare you to go see the rest of the world at least once so that you can understand God's global plan.

Commitment While most excuses for abstaining from missions fall into the categories of comfort or circumstances, I do believe that one category still remains that must be addressed that keeps many people from going to the world:

1. *"I simply don't have God's heart for lost people."* While no one readily admits this statement in Christian circles, I challenge you to evaluate yourself and see if this is genuinely the cause of your hesitancy. I was here once. I didn't care about God's global agenda. I understood that lost people were all over the world, but I did not see it as my personal responsibility to do anything about it.

John wrote that since Jesus Christ laid down his life for us, we ought to lay our lives down for others (1 John 3:16). I decided not to wait for a compassionate heart to develop for the nations, I simply decided to go. It was a biblical command; I was a follower of Christ, and the rest is history. I didn't understand God's heart until I followed his example. My obedience led me to the corresponding understanding. When I followed Christ around the world in college, God broke my heart with the needs of the world, and I could never ever be the same again.

Most college students implicitly respond to the Great Commission that once they get everything in their lives squared away, then they will follow Jesus to the nations. If you are waiting for the perfect time in your life to follow Jesus, life has just passed you by - He *is* our life (Col. 3:4). Our purpose is to go. We are not called to wait for some abstract time when everything in our little world gets settled. Our call is to make disciples of all nations, not to make our lives comfortable. When we neglect God's first call on our lives, we find ourselves disturbingly discontented and restless. The longing God put in our hearts is not to establish large bank accounts or to climb the corporate ladder to success, God has lavished us with grace so fully that we should feel compelled to go wherever and whenever he calls.

Jesus was constantly approached by potential followers in his personal ministry on earth. As prospects would verbally declare their commitment, Jesus had an amazing knack at striking straight at their underlying intentions. In one certain incident, Jesus was approached by many would-be followers (Luke 9:57-62). Jesus informed those listening that if they were looking for a comfortable, spiritual ride, they were following the wrong guy. If they were waiting to get all their issues in their lives settled, they would never go. The only perfect time to follow Jesus is right now.

There is no looking back. When you start this work of following Jesus, you are never to look behind you dreaming of another path (Luke 9:62). The biggest issue of following Christ to the nations is not of comfort or circumstances, we simply lack the commitment that Christ deserves.

The Perfect Time

In college, you now have a better opportunity to follow Christ to the nations than you will ever have in your entire life. You have enough freedom from your family, and you lack full-time job status just yet. Most of you do not have responsibilities to a spouse or a child yet, and you do not have as many bills now as you one day will have (I know that might be hard to believe but it is true). If you ever wanted a perfect time to get your feet wet and try a short term missions experience, it is right now.

To get started, I would recommend that you inquire at your church or a local college ministry about possible mission opportunities for this summer. You can go by yourself or as a member of a team. You could travel almost anywhere and do almost anything, but you must commit to go somewhere. Five years from now, your responsibilities will be so much more intense. You will not have the luxury of a summer break. You will not have the ability to go to the nations so easily when you have a mortgage and a family of your own. Find a list of opportunities, pray through them, and apply for one that sets your heart on fire as you read through the description.

Another benefit of going on a short term trip is that you get to see if God has been molding you for a longer missionary commitment. Every college team I have ever taken on the foreign mission field always comes back with at least one person indicating that God has called him to the nations for a lifetime. The rest of the team always walks away knowing that foreign missions will be some integral part of their lives from that point forward. You will not be able to go to the nations and come back the same.

I could fill up these pages with those unforgettable moments I spent in college on the mission field. I wish I had room to tell you about being taken into custody in a closed country and swallowing a map in order to keep missionaries safe. If pages would allow, I would tell you about a young girl I renamed "Naomi" who was ashamed that in a closed country she had only led sixty of her friends to Christ in her first six months of being a Christian. I wish you could have been with me as my team sang worship songs in a closed country and someone asked us why we sang with such passion and what was the reason for our hope. God has done so much in the nations, and I have been blessed to witness a small fraction of it.

In order to close this chapter, I want to tell you one story about a friend named Yoshi that I met in Japan. At Hitsobashi University, my team was conducting English clubs at lunchtime for students who wanted to improve their linguistic skills. We would sing American songs for them, and they would show us their artwork. We talked about American customs and played games with those students. They tricked me into eating sushi that was layered with so much wasabi that I beat my fastest track speed as I ran to the water fountain.

One day, we did a mime (yes, I did a mime, but we spoke different languages; I didn't have a choice) that showed Christ's love for sinners and our constant rebellion against him. The college students found the sketch humorous until the point where this great guy in the story was killed by these pretty rotten characters. As we finished the mime, we broke into groups to work on English and to talk about what they had just seen.

The conversations took a long time as these students were attempting to select the correct English phrases in order not to embarrass themselves. As we struggled through that conversation, my buddy Yoshi asked me who the main character in the mime was. I told him that the actor was portraying the person of Jesus.

Then he asked me the question that I still haven't gotten over even to this day. Everything changed for me as he slowly struggled to pronounce these English words: "Who is Jesus?"

I normally have answers for people when asked a question. At that moment, I was speechless. How do you begin to describe the one who has flipped your life upside down? How do you express the type of love displayed at the cross to someone who has never even heard the story? Most importantly, why hadn't Yoshi ever even heard the name Jesus? He was twenty-one years old, and he had never heard the name of the only one who can truly save someone. Then I finally understood why he had never heard the name Jesus – because I had been unwilling to go (Rom. 10:14-15).

As I apathetically wasted away at my Christian college with my four Bibles on my dorm room shelves, people were dying without ever hearing even the name of Jesus. I could never be the same. I was about to engage in something I had never experienced - I had the privileged opportunity to introduce someone for the first time to the person of Jesus.

With tears welling up in my eyes, I replied, "Yoshi, Jesus is my everything. He is my reason for living. He was sent by God to rescue us from the hopelessness of this world. He lived a perfect life because we couldn't do it. We couldn't reach God, so God reached out to us. All the bad things that you and I have done in our lives, Christ took the punishment on the cross in our places. He rose again. Death couldn't defeat him; the grave couldn't contain him. Jesus Christ came back to life defeating sin and death once and for all.

"Yoshi, he loves you and he doesn't want you to buy into the lie that you can make it to God based on your own merit. You need to turn your life over to him."

Yoshi asked some more questions about Jesus, and I just kept on bragging about who Jesus is and how he had changed my life. Out of nowhere, he asked me questions about American life. I didn't want to change the subject, but he kept asking me questions about the privileged life that he saw on the news about American college students. He finally got to the point when he asked, "If you have all those wonderful things in America and at your college, then why would you leave and come to this country for your summer vacation?"

I replied, "Because Jesus Christ loves you very much. I would leave my country anytime that it meant I got to tell you how much you are loved by God."

That day, as I presented the gospel to those Japanese students, I was reminded of a letter that a youth in my church had given me before I got on the plane. In that letter, she stated, "What an honor it must be to go and tell people about Jesus who will hear about him for the first time through you. God must think very highly of you to give you the same opportunity he gave to his disciples. You are very lucky."

We really are. Will you go? Will you ever experience the life-changing moment of being present when someone hears the name of Jesus for the first time. I promise, you will never ever be the same.

Group Questions

Chapter 14: the World

*The Great Commission is not a suggestion to be considered,
but a commandment to be obeyed.*

1. Which of the ten excuses presented are on the top of your list?

2. If someone is worried about his or her comfort on the mission field, how would you respond to that person?

3. Will there ever be a time in your life when all your circumstances perfectly enable you to go to the mission field? Why?

4. Read 2 Corinthians 5:16-21. Who does Paul classify as ambassadors?

5. What could be your first step to follow Christ around the world?

Pray that God gives you his heart for the nations. Pray that his heart will propel you to go.

the **Will**

You find God's will by doing God's will.

Towards the end of my college career, I started noticing something about myself: I was getting old. While I graduated at twenty-one years old, signs of aging were starting to reveal themselves regularly. Instead of sleeping straight through the night without a hitch, I began to wake up at different times throughout the night thinking about the uncertainties concerning post-graduation life. Upon realization of the upcoming bills awaiting me, I became a legitimate cheapskate not wanting to spend my own earned money as fast as I had spent someone else's earned money.

One of the worst things I noticed about aging my senior year was my increasing level of forgetfulness. I would call someone's cell phone but forget whom I had dialed by the second ring. I would walk out of class forgetting the assignment just given. I would intentionally visit a guy's dorm room for a specific purpose, but by the time I got there, I had forgotten the reason for which I came. It was so embarrassing to leave a place without accomplishing the reasons for which you came.

I'm fearful about that for my life too. I am scared to death to think that God put me on this earth for a specific purpose, and I simply miss it. In chapter one, I discussed the ordeal of losing my watch. I mentioned how those feelings were similar to what many people would feel when this life was over. Having to face God and admit that I wasted my one life is not a scenario I would eagerly hope to experience. As this book comes to a close, I think it is critical to remind you once again that you must decide to make Jesus your one thing for which you live. If he is your one thing, then you must relentlessly seek what his will is for your life.

You do not want to enter heaven without what he asked you to get during your time on earth. You do not want to admit that you missed the purpose for which he created you. Paul wrote of King David that after he had served the purpose of God in his own generation, he died (Acts 13:36). Not before and not after, but once David had checked off the reason for which God had him on this earth, there was no further reason to keep him around this side of eternity.

Unfortunately, that is not everyone's story. I am quite afraid that I will die before I serve the purpose of God in my own generation. I am fearful that I will exhaust myself in attempts to earn a large amount of money, gain a significant amount of influence, build a pretty impressive reputation, and purchase a whole bunch of trivial earthly possessions. In my attempts, I could easily miss out on why God had me on earth. I can hear him say, "Son, that is great that you accumulated a whole bunch of stuff down there, but did you realize that you cannot bring it here with you? A lot of people told you, 'Well done,' but you are not going to hear that from me. You were very busy during your life, but you never accomplished the purpose for which I sent you."

Misconceptions

Many people have misconceptions of God. Misconceptions of God lead to misconceptions concerning his will. Many college students speak of the desire to know God's will as if it is an impossible task since God will probably not oblige. An incorrect theology leads to an incorrect belief concerning his will. Think about this: God wants you to know his will more than you want to know his will. It's his will, don't you think he wants you to know it and fulfill it? Unfortunately, some people think his will is not that easy to find.

Disguised Will. Some people believe that God gives a disguised will. As God overlooks all of creation, he finds pleasure in disguising his will for his children. Like a mischievous entity in the sky, the belief in this God pictures him hiding his will from his children. When you get near finding it, he moves it to another spot. When you think you will find it in a certain location, it is nowhere to be found. Some people honestly think that God finds enjoyment out of making his children guess where his will is.

Dreaded Will. Other people think that God's will for their lives will be something to dread. If you imagined what would be the absolute worst scenario for your life, what would it be? Whatever came to your mind, that is God's will for you. Many college students think that if they ask God for his will, they are going to be a single missionary living in a hut in Africa with no access to Starbucks or text messaging (since it can't get worse than that, right?). Many students think that God has a will for them that is to be dreaded, and they forget that God our Father knows how to give incredible gifts to his children (Matt. 7:11).

Drastic Will. Some people await God's will to appear drastically. As you walk along the road one day, the clouds will break open, sunbeams will burst forth from the sky, and through the right amount of sunlight and cloud blockage, you will be able to read on the road the name of the person you are to marry, the major with which you will graduate, and the job you will receive after college. While God does speak in drastic ways at times, we forget that God also speaks through circumstances, passions, and opportunities. Often, I believe God wants us to use the wisdom he has giving us to make a godly decision. I think beyond these three possibilities, God has another option.

Delightful Will. Amazingly, God does have a will for your life, and it is not that bad honestly. King David wrote that we are to delight ourselves in the Lord, and he will give us the desires of our heart (Ps. 37:4). If we really are attempting to put on weight by being biblically obedient in every area of our lives, God earnestly desires to give us the desires of our hearts. If you are honestly delighting God, your desires will not be selfish. God's reign in your life will be so complete that your desires will actually conform to his desires. In this state, you will have passions to do a certain something, and it's a good chance that you are possessing a God-given desire. In your obedience, your heart may beat wildly for another person, and you can safely assume that you are in line with God.

When you are walking in step with God's commands, you will experience the peace associated with God's plan.

Paul instructed the Ephesian Christians to walk in a wise manner. He urged them to make the best possible use of their time in order not to miss out on the opportunity of this life. Understanding that life is short, Paul exhorted them not to waste their lives in evil manners. He then states that Christians are to seek to understand what the will of the Lord is (Eph. 5:15-17). Knowing God's will is a noteworthy ambition. To know God's will, you must possess an internal desire to find it. God says that we can find him when we seek for him with all of our hearts (Jer. 29:13). Percentages will not succeed here; we must desire to find him and his will with every ounce of our being.

If you believe that God does have a delightful will, you probably are now just curious with what that will actually is. As you are nearing graduation, you want to know the answers to the most poignant questions in your life right now. In order to know God's will, you must first realize that we know parts of God's will as secure and parts of it as unsure. All of God's will is knowable, but some parts of his will are firmly secure, and there is no need to seek any further. Some of his will is not plainly obvious, and our unsure state will cause us to seek further. You find God's will by doing God's will.

Secure Part

When I worked on an assembly line one summer during college, I learned the significance concerning quotas. Each Monday morning, I would put my gloves and goggles on, and I would receive a quota of bottom sashes for skylights that needed to be completed by Friday. If I could not produce the quota of skylights, I put other workers behind or had the possibility of having to work on that Saturday. We did not receive a new quota until the first quota was done. All I had to worry about was the number that had been given me by my boss. It would have been foolish to ask my boss if I could work on next week's assignment when this week's had not been completed yet. I didn't get a new assignment until I had completed what had already been given me.

God's will is a lot like that. Most college students eagerly seek to discover God's will concerning a job or a mate, but they fail to realize that God has already given them assignments that they have not yet completed. Why would God give you a new assignment if you have not completed the ones he has already given you?

Do you realize all that God has already asked of you? Have you given thanks in all circumstances (1 Thess. 5:18)? Do you bear others' burdens (Gal. 6:10)? When was the last time you met the practical needs of others (James 2:14-16)? The problem is not that we are ignorant concerning God's will. The problem is that we don't like it.

We do not delight in God's secure will. God has provided us with non-negotiables present in his Word that he wants us to pursue actively, and we would honestly prefer to wait for a new assignment. We want God to reveal his will concerning our desire at revenge, but he has already commanded us to love our enemies and pray for those persecuting us (Matt. 5:44). We wait for God to give us a sign to witness to our suite mate, but why would we make him repeat himself (Col. 4:5-6)? We waste time praying about whether or not we should confront another Christian straying when God has already made it perfectly clear (Matt. 18:15). We are not unaware of God's will, we just struggle with being obedient to it. Without a doubt, God's Word provides the secure portion of God's will. In five specific places, the Bible makes it crystal clear concerning his will for you.

Saved. One element of God's will that is extremely clear is that you become saved. Paul wrote that God's will was that everyone be saved and to come to a knowledge of the truth (1 Tim. 2:3-4). If you are reading this book and unsure of your personal relationship with Jesus, God's will is that you cover this portion first. If you understand that a holy God set up rules for us to live by, and we sinned by transgressing against his law, then you must realize that God would have to find a way for us to salvation. He sent Jesus to bear the punishment of our sins, and if we confess with our mouths that Jesus is Lord and believe in our hearts that God raised him from the dead, we can be saved (Rom. 10:9). God's will for you is that you be forgiven of your sins and be reconciled to God.

Sanctified. God's explicit will is that you also be sanctified (1 Thess. 4:3). When you become a Christian, God justifies you once and for all. That means that you are not guilty anymore in his eyes. When we die, God's Word teaches us that we will be glorified as we go into eternity with him. From the time of justification until the time of glorification, God's will is that you be busy in the process of sanctification. To be sanctified means that you are continually transforming more into the image of Christ. You constantly ask God to investigate areas in your life (Ps. 139:23) and allow him to continue working on you (Phil. 1:6).

Spirit-Filled. In the secure part of God's will, he also desires that you be Spirit-filled (Eph. 5:17-18). As we studied this passage earlier in this chapter, you may remember that Paul instructed that the wise way to live was to understand the will of God. He continues to say not to get drunk with wine, but be filled with the Spirit instead. God's desire is that you be led daily by the influence of his Holy Spirit. I always desired to experience walking beside the physical presence of Jesus like the disciples. Surprisingly, Jesus stated that it is to our advantage that we do not walk with Jesus physically but rather be led by the Spirit inwardly (John 16:7). Jesus taught that a Spirit-filled life would be more life-changing than physically walking with the Savior!

Suffering. Another secure portion of God's will is his promise that we suffer. This promise is not as appealing as the others, but it is nonetheless God's will. Peter wrote that all people in this world would suffer, but he recommended that we suffer for doing good rather than doing evil (1 Pet. 3:17). Everyone will suffer due to differing causes. Some people will suffer in this life due to unwise decisions that they make. Their actions simply bring about a cause and effect natural to the makeup of our world. Christians, on the other hand, are to suffer for living godly. If we are to suffer, God's will is that we suffer at the hands of people hostile towards God. In alignment with him, that suffering is worthy suffering. Unworthy suffering that our mistakes bring upon ourselves is not honoring to God.

Sacrificial. By refusing to be conformed to this world and choosing to be transformed by the renewing of our minds, God's will is that we live in such a manner that we glorify him in all of our actions

(Rom. 12:1-2). Paul states that a sacrificial Christian, offering his or her life as a lifestyle of worship, should be able to discern God's will. If this Christian is actively laying his life down for Christ everyday (Luke 9:23), he will be able to discern those areas in which he is unsure about God's will.

 The second part of God's will is those unsure areas. These are the areas for which the Bible is not explicit. You will not discover in Habakkuk 3:4 if you are supposed to date Josh or Brooks. 2 Corinthians 2:14 does not inform you of what major you should declare. Unfortunately, Leviticus does not include any specific words about what you should do this summer.

What are we to do about those areas in which we are unsure? How do we discern those grey areas in which God has not given explicit instruction? Taking wisdom from Scripture, I have learned to apply the ABC's of God's will to many situations. This framework is a good checkpoint to see if what you are feeling is in line with God's heart.

Ambition. Why do you want to do what you want to do? Before making a big decision, I often probe to discover my ambition. If I can find the true reasoning for why I want to do what I want to do, I can often find out if it is God's will or not.

Normally, most of the unsure areas of God's will presents two choices: a chance to build my kingdom or a chance to build God's Kingdom. When I am confronted with a decision, oftentimes, I am being presented an option to promote Christ or myself. If I have impure motives, I normally can spot them by seeking my ambition in this decision.

By spending time with God and questioning my ambition, I have discovered some pretty harsh realities. God has shown me areas in which my desires were completely selfish in nature. At other times, he has shown me that those passions I had in my heart were given from him, and I needed to act upon them. Regardless of the situation, once I allow God to investigate my heart, I am able to truly ascertain my ambition.

Bible. After I have checked my ambition, I then turn to the Bible. While an explicit word for my situation may not be present, oftentimes, I am able to find a biblical principle that helps me in my deliberation. As I seek God's Word, I am able to discover his heart for similar situations, and I am able to make a better informed decision.

When I found a great mission opportunity my sophomore year of college, I went down my dorm hall and asked the guys to pray about an opportunity to go into a closed country and share the gospel. As I engaged most of the guys, they assured me they would make the trip a matter of prayer and told me they would get back with me. When I presented the opportunity to my friend Adam, he quickly responded that he would go. I reminded him the necessity of prayer in such a major spiritual decision and he replied, "God has already said in his Word to go into all nations, why do I need to ask him to repeat those instructions to me?"

As I left his room, I understood God's will a lot better. While the Bible does not include a command for Adam to travel to that specific country that specific year, he was able to take the commands of Scripture and apply the principles into his own life. Like Adam, I implore you to search for biblical commands and principles that you can apply to these unsure areas of God's commands.

Counsel. After I have probed my ambition and delved into the pages of Scripture, I will seek out godly counsel as a last resort. I put counsel as a last resort because most people unfortunately reorder this whole process. When a dilemma arises, most people run to a spiritual mentor and ask his or her opinion on the matter at hand. While I am thankful for those mentors in our lives, I firmly believe that the unsure areas of our lives are often an invitation from God to go deeper in our relationship with him.

> God sometimes puts unclear options in our path to provoke us to get on our knees and into his Word.

If you run to your pastor to gain his wisdom, you bypass the tension that God graciously provided. God sometimes puts unclear options in our path to provoke us to get on our knees and into his Word. When we bypass these faith-stretching opportunities, we miss the blessing of drawing near to Jesus in the midst of these unsure areas of God's will.

Only after you have examined your ambition and studied God's Word should you go find some counsel. If after much prayer and study you still find yourself unsure about a decision, it is recommended that you find good, godly counsel. Find someone who has Jesus' best interest in mind. Do not find someone who has your best interest in mind. Oftentimes, those people can care more for our comfort than our obedience. Find someone whose commitment is first and foremost dedicated to the glory of God, and present the situation to that counselor. Once this spiritual mentor has provided you with advice, make sure that you weigh it against God's truths.

After all this hard work, you might face some decisions of which you are still unsure. If you arrive at this juncture, sometimes you have to simply make the wisest call you can make. In making this type of decision, refrain from taking God's name in vain. If you are not completely sure that God is leading you, do not blanket your actions with the statement, "God told me to..."

Many people have done some pretty ridiculous things and blamed God for it. I have also heard people often claim that Jesus told them to be a missionary, and later Jesus told them to be a CEO. Either Jesus is schizophrenic or someone is using God's name in vain. In those moments when you lack 100% certainty on a decision, be bold enough to say, "I believe God is leading me in this direction, and therefore, I have chosen to do..."

In those moments, ask God to shut the door in order to keep you out of what is not his will. While you may desire God's plan for the rest of your life right now, remember that God wants to keep you close more than he wants to keep you informed. You are on a need-to-know basis. If he educated you right now concerning who you were to marry, where you would work, and how much money you would make, you probably would no longer seek him as fervently as you do right now. Your information would keep you from staying close. Remember that God's Word is a lamp to your feet and a light to your path (Ps. 119:105), and not a flood lamp for the next mile. By showing you just enough light for solely the next step, God is not being mysterious, he is just ensuring your commitment to seeking him for the long haul which is in your best interest.

In college, one of my best friend's father was an evangelist.   Rick would travel to different churches attempting to lead people to Christ and lead Christians to deeper levels of commitment. He once told me of a particular service that changed my life forever.

In one particular church in which he was preaching, the pastor was expected to meet the congregation at the back door to shake their hands as they exited. Most members commented on what a nice job he had done with the message and then move towards their vehicles. At this church, an older man lingered at the back of the line in hope to spend some quality time with Rick.

As this feeble man hobbled over to Rick, he shook Rick's hand and encouraged him concerning his message delivery. Rick thanked him, but this man would not quit shaking his hand. As Rick began to get a little uncomfortable at why this man would not let his hand go, the man finally began to explain his situation.

"Preacher Rick, I heard a message like the one you gave tonight when I was in college. A preacher just like you told us young people that we needed to follow God's will. We needed to reach out to the world and make something of ourselves. That night, I told God I would do anything he asked of me. I'd go anywhere and do anything."

Rick replied, "Well, that is great. And so what did you do?"

With tears streaming down his cheeks, this old man replied, "Absolutely nothing. I have wasted my life. I knew God's will for my life at one time, but I completely went in the opposition direction, and now I don't have many more years to live, and I can't ever get them back."

Hearing about that conversation in college changed me. I could no longer be the same. I did not want to be aware of God's will for my life in college only to walk away from it upon graduation. I did not want to arrive at heaven and tell God that I lost the precious gift of this life he gave me. I wanted to know that I counted for something.

I pray that you give Jesus glory concerning obeying his will for your life. I hope that you do not buy into the lie in college that anything is better than Jesus. I pray that you don't settle for shortcuts or reach a level of apathy walking with Jesus. I pray that you make him your one thing in college and for the rest of your life. I pray that you strive for biblical obedience in all these other pivotal areas mentioned. I pray that at the end of your life, you can say that your time in college was spent growing closer to Jesus, and you never looked back.

Let's face it, you will gain the freshman fifteen in college. You will give glory to something. I just hope you put it on in all the right places. I hope you give it all to Jesus.

Group Questions

Chapter 15: the Will
You find God's will by doing God's will.

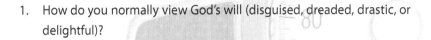

1. How do you normally view God's will (disguised, dreaded, drastic, or delightful)?

2. Is there any part of God's will that he has already revealed to you that you have not completed yet?

3. When you normally attempt to discern God's will, which area do you investigate first (ambition, Bible, or counsel)?

4. Read Ephesians 5:15-17. Why would God want you to know his will?

5. Is there any areas in which you need to seek your own personal ambition and the Bible concerning God's will?

Pray that you embrace God's will. Commit to him that you want your life to count for the purposes for which he purchased it.

About the Author

Travis Agnew is a Christian, husband, father, worship pastor, preacher, religion instructor, songwriter, author, student, and blogger. If he gets any more specific, his status could have probably changed by the time you read this section. So if you want any information on him or his ministry, the easiest way to find out more is to visit travisagnew.org.

travisagnew.org